Carbon Shinai
カーボンシナイ

- CF-Type
- DB-Type
- K1-Type
- K2-Type

Orange　Red　Yellow

We have improved the official Carbon Shinai rubber stopper.

The NEW official rubber stopper.
¥300 (domestic Japanese price)

WARNING!! Never use anything other than our official rubber stopper on your Carbon Shinai !!

When using your Carbon Shinai.....

1. To prevent injury, please use our official rubber stopper. Do not use stoppers made for conventional bamboo shinai on your Carbon Shinai, as there is a risk of injury to your opponent if the tip breaks through and enters their men grill.

2. When choosing a sakigawa (leather tip), make sure that it is more than 5cm in length and completely covers our rubber stopper. If the sakigawa is shorter than 5cm, there is a risk of injury to your opponent if a slat slips out and enters their men grill.

3. Do not shave the plastic surface of your Carbon Shinai. If you shave the surface, the black carbon fiber will be exposed, causing damage that may result in injury to your opponent.

4. Always check the condition of the surface of your Carbon Shinai before and during use. As soon as you notice any cracks, or peeling of the surface, or if black carbon fiber is exposed on any part of the outside, inside or edges of the Shinai, or you notice any other damage, stop using the shinai immediately. There is a danger of injury to your opponent if your Carbon Shinai is split or broken.

5. When tying the nakayui (leather binding), either tie a knot in the tsuru-ito (cord), or tie one end of the nakayui to the tsuru-ito, or by another means ensuring that is does not move up and down during use. If there is any damage whatsoever to the sakigawa, tsukagawa (hilt), rubber stopper, tsuru-ito and so on, replace them immediately.

6. If the tip of the Carbon Shinai is damaged, or a slat is protuding out of the sakigawa, there is a danger that it could enter your opponent's men grill and injure them.

Kendogu Revolution

Mu-Jun Men
武楯面

WARNING!!

1. Under no circumstances should organic solvents (such as thinner, alcohol, benzene, toluene, acetone, gasoline, kerosene, etc.), acidic or alkali chemicals, domestic cleansers, car cleansers, or anti-mist sprays, be used to clean the shield. These substances will cause the shield to deteriorate, leading to clouding, cracking or breaking, thereby resulting in danger of injury to the face.

2. Should the shield develop deep scratches or cracks on either the outer or inner surface, discontinue use of the shield immediately, and replace it with an undamaged shield. If the shield is used in such a condition, there is a danger of it breaking, causing injury to the face.

3. It should be fully understood that, as with the traditional Japanese Kendo-Men (mask), there is still the danger of injury to the face through fragments of broken bamboo or Carbon Shinai pieces penetrating through areas not covered by the shield.

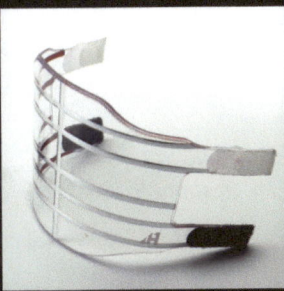

SG-Type

- SCIENCE TO SEEK SAFETY -

HASEGAWA
HASEGAWA CORPORATION

WEB : http://kendo.hasegawakagaku.co.jp/
Email : contact@hasegawakagaku.co.jp

Carbon Shinai — Points to be checked

DANGER !!   **ATTENTION !!**

Before these happen.....

Although the Carbon Shinai is much more durable than a conventional bamboo one, it will inevitably become damaged since it is a sword that is used to repeatedly strike and thrust your opponent. Therefore, inspect the condition of the surface, sides or reverse of the Carbon Shinai's slats before, during and after use, and stop using it immediately should damage like in the following pictures be observed. (These pictures are just a few examples of many.)

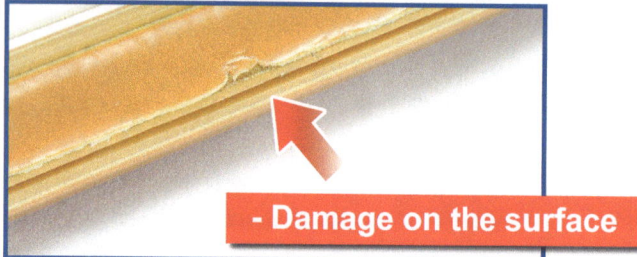

- Damage on the surface

- An unglued surface sheet

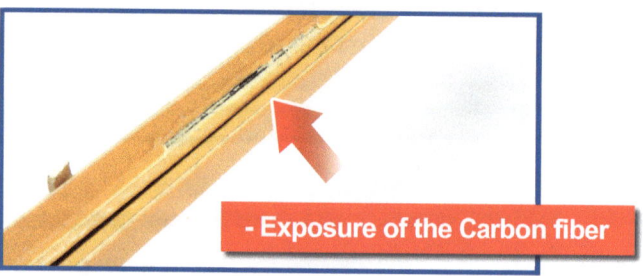

- Exposure of the Carbon fiber

- Longitudinal crack on the surface

- Damage and ungluing of the surface

- Crack on the reverse

There is the case where the reverse gets cracked even without any damage on the surface. Inspect the inside of the Shinai by pushing the pieces with the fingers and unbinding the Naka-yui.

HASEGAWA-KOTE

- Detachable and washable "Tenouchi" is easy to wash and dry.

- "Tenouchi" is replaceable when torn. No need to repair.

Kote (Main part)

Tenouchi (Inner)

- SCIENCE TO SEEK SAFETY -

HASEGAWA

HASEGAWA CORPORATION
http://kendo.hasegawakagaku.co.jp/

KENDO WORLD Volume 7.2 June 2014 Contents

Editorial	2
Miyako Tanaka Price	4
Hanshi Says Taba Norinobu (Hanshi 8-dan)	5
Embrace the Failing	7
Grading Successfully: Part 2 Shigematsu Kimiaki (Kyoshi 8-dan)	10
FIK Anti-Doping Compliance	15
The Nuts 'n' Bolts of Kendo All about Shiai	16
The 14th Hong Kong Asian Open Kendo Championships	20
Reidan-jichi Part 17 Kihon Dōsa No. 6	24
sWords of Wisdom "Shōbu wa saya no uchi"	26
Kendo in the Snow	28
An Innovative Method for Kendo Shiai: Bringing out the Best	30
What's this about the new rules for blocking?	32
Kendo That Cultivates People Part 16 Teaching Kendo to the Next Generation	34
Film Review Uzumasa Limelight	42
Historical Oddities The Works of Tetsuya Noguchi	44
Book Review HAGAKURE	48
Shinai Sagas The Champion	50
Naginata Monbushō Seitei Kata	55
Strategy for NITO PART 8	77
'A Man of Many Parts' Portrait of an Inimitable Swordsman	86
An Oasis of Equality in the Male-Dominated World of Sport? Finnish Women's Experience of Kendo	93
Book Review GoGo Ninja	97

Kendo World Staff
- Bunkasha International President & Editor-in-Chief— Alex Bennett PhD
- Bunkasha International Vice President & Assistant Editor— Michael Ishimatsu-Prime MA
- Bunkasha International Vice President & Graphic Design— Shishikura 'Kan' Masashi
- Bunkasha International Vice President— Hamish Robison
- Bunkasha International Vice President— Michael Komoto MA
- Bunkasha International General Manager— Baptiste Tavernier MA
- Senior Consultants— Yonemoto Masayuki, Shima Masahiko

KW Staff Writers / Translators / Photographers / Graphic Designer / Sub-editors
- Axel Pilgrim PhD
- Blake Bennett MA
- Bruce Flanagan MA
- Bryan Peterson
- Charlie Kondek
- Gabriel Weitzner
- Honda Sōtarō PhD
- Imafuji Masahiro MBA
- Jeff Broderick
- Kate Sylvester MA
- Lockie Jackson PhD
- Miho Maki
- Paul Benson
- Scott Huegel (MaSC)
- Sergio Boffa PhD
- Stephen Nagy PhD
- Steven Harwood MA
- Stuart Gibson
- Taylor Winter
- Tony Cundy
- Trevor Jones
- Tyler Rothmar
- Yamaguchi Remi
- Vivian Yung

KW would like to thank the following people and organisations for their valuable cooperation:
- All Japan Kendo Federation
- All Japan Budogu
- Hasegawa Teiichi - President, Hasegawa Corporation
- *Kendo Jidai* Magazine
- *Kendo Nihon* Magazine
- Nippon Budokan Foundation
- Shogun Kendogu
- TOZANDO

Guest Writers
- Andy Fisher (All Japan Budogu, British National Team)
- Bando Takao (Kendo K7-dan, Prof. Osaka University)
- Boris Jansen (Kendo 6-dan, Netherlands National Team)
- Daryl Tong, (Assoc. Prof. Otago University)
- Kihara Motohiro (Kendo K7-dan, Prof. Naruto University of Education)
- Kurt Schmucker (U.S. Naginata Federation, Vice President)
- Kusama Masurao (Hiroshima University)
- Magnus Johansson (Shimbukan Skelleftea Budo Club)
- Nakano Yasoji (Now deceased. Kendo Hanshi 9-dan)
- Ōya Minoru (Prof. International Budo University; Kendo Kyōshi 7-dan)
- Paul Budden (Kendo K7-dan, Kodokan Kendo U.K.)
- Rita Deksnyte (Sports Psychology Counselor, Lithuania)
- Shigematsu Kimiaki (Kendo Kyōshi 8-dan)
- Sumi Masatake (Kendo Hanshi 8-dan)
- Taba Norinobu (Kendo Hanshi 8-dan)
- Yamaguchi Masato (Nitō practitioner)
- Yokoyama Naoya (Yokohama National University)

COPYRIGHT 2014 Bunkasha International Corporation. No part of this publication may be reproduced in any form whatsoever without written permission from the publisher, except by writers who are permitted to quote brief passages for the purpose of review or reference. Kindly contact Bunkasha International Corporation at info@kendo-world.com.

Editorial Conventions Used in KW Inevitably in a magazine of this nature, many non-English words appear in the text. All Japanese words are italicised and include macrons (ū, ō) etc., apart from common place names and nouns, and words in some captions and headings. As a general exception, KW treats all the martial arts (budo), such as kendo, iaido, jodo, ranks, and so on as Anglicised words without using macrons. Japanese names are written in accordance to the traditional Japanese manner of family name followed by given name. Traditional *ryūha* are written with capitals and therefore are not italicised. 'Kata' with a capital 'K' refers to the set of Nippon Kendo Kata, and *kata* refers to set forms in general. The masculine personal pronoun is used throughout the text in some articles in the interest of readability, and is in no way meant to slight the significant contributions made by female kendoka.

Editorial Alex Bennett

"The way of the kendoka is to be found in dying…"

Recently, I published a translation of the bushido classic *Hagakure*—"The way of the warrior is to be found in dying…" Although I have spent the majority of my adult life researching the rather nebulous field of bushido, I have always been mindful not to fall too deeply into the "wannabe samurai" camp so prevalent among beguiled Japanophiles. I obviously like the subject (a lot) as an academic pursuit, but I never intended to be an inductee into the church of bushido. On the other hand, being a hard-boiled kendoka, I am probably a little more open minded to the potential usefulness of samurai wisdom than the typical Western scholar on the subject, and am thus undoubtedly more ensconced in the church than I care to admit.

I have written a number of books in Japanese on the subject, and seem to have eked out a niche market of sorts. Being the foreigner who has researched bushido for two doctoral dissertations, who has actually done kendo for close to three decades, and who cannot be accused of being a right-wing ultranationalist, Japanese people are typically curious about my take on things. The observations in my writings are generally accepted as a "neutral", "rational", and "fair" acclamation of traditional Japanese ideals that the natives have largely forsaken… "If a foreigner who knows his stuff reckons it's good, then maybe we Japanese should reconsider the value of our unique traditional culture…"

Hey, whatever sells books is fine with me. Although I'm certainly not blindly fanatical about what I (or others) spin regarding bushido, I'm finding that my cautious, analytical cynicism, requisite for any scholar worth his or her salt, is beginning to soften somewhat as my understanding of kendo advances. In this sense, translating *Hagakure* turned out to be quite a journey, with more than a few "I totally get it!" revelations along the way. I suspect that I forged a closer, or at least a different kind of affinity to the content and its author than other translators, or even most Japanese readers, simply because I do kendo every day. The ultimate bushido fieldwork…

Hagakure is often misunderstood both in and outside of Japan. With contextualization, however, it serves as a fascinating window on the trials and tribulations of the samurai lifestyle during the Tokugawa period. *Hagakure* was completed in 1716, and this was a time in which the martial arts were undergoing a significant transformation in terms of form, objectives, philosophy, and rationale. Although not associated directly with martial arts practice per se, many of the dictums in *Hagakure* do provide an intriguing backdrop to key concepts espoused in modern kendo.

One such concept is that of "*sutemi*". Literally to "discard one's body", this is the mental and physical state of total commitment in giving something one's all. In kendo, this amounts to attempting a single blow with everything you have got, without concern for the outcome. In essence, it is to execute each technique with self-sacrificial drive and indifference to personal safety. No warrior was more fearsome, the samurai believed, than one who cared not for his own life or safety in the thick of battle. No kendoka is more likely to succeed than one who can launch into an attack without being constrained by shackles of doubt or trepidation about the outcome. "Fools jump where angels fear to tread", the old adage goes. Kendoka are no angels anyway, but there are times when you've just gotta jump. That's really the point to our training—honing our gut instinct to know precisely when it is not foolish to jump in and seize the moment.

The pages of *Hagakure* abound with teachings pointing to the importance of this mindset in daily life. For example, "A heroic warrior (*kusemono*) does not concern himself with victory or defeat. Without hesitating, he whips himself into a deadly fury (*shini-gurui*). This is when he understands; this is when he awakens from the dream." (1–55) In this case, the stalwart warrior finds spiritual liberation by detaching himself from concerns of winning or losing. Ultimately, he will prevail over others who are more "calculated" in their approach to gaining a favourable result. "Just do it!" *Hagakure* advises.

One of my favourite anecdotes demonstrating this point concerns a party of blind monks attempting to traverse a treacherous mountain pass. "As they passed around the top of a cliff, their legs began to tremble, and although they took extreme care, they were overcome by fear. The leader staggered and then fell off the edge. The rest all cried, 'Oh what a terrible end!' They were unable to take a step further. The blind monk who had fallen off the cliff yelled up from below: 'Do not be frightened. Falling was not so bad. I am now quite unperturbed. I worried about what would happen if I fell, and was somewhat apprehensive. But now I am very calm. If you want to put your minds at ease, quickly fall [and get it over with].'" (10–125)

For some reason, this anecdote conjures up images of a possible Monty Python skit involving a whole lot of monks jumping off a cliff to lose their fear of falling. Again though, that is pretty much what we are encouraged to do in kendo, and once that fear is gone, it is quite liberating indeed.

Sutemi is the requisite mental attitude in all budo in which the practitioner ideally commits body and soul into the attack in an act of total self-denial and sacrifice, with no concern for the aftermath. What will be, will be. Although nobody fights with swords anymore, such philosophical and spiritual underpinnings remain an important feature in kendo. In this context, kendo is a precious legacy left by samurai, who sought strength to confront and accept their mortality at every living moment through their training. At least, that was the ideal. Their accumulated experience and wisdom can actually provide modern kendo practitioners with potent insights into the beauty of life, and how to live to one's full potential, paradoxically based on the *sutemi* ideal of self-annihilation. *Hagakure* demonstrates this point beautifully, especially if you have a reference point through your kendo involvement.

The laborious task of translating *Hagakure* gave me a new appreciation of the many "cosmic" and seemingly "reckless" teachings imparted to us rather tenuously in the dojo on a regular basis. Ironically, "throwing it all away" often results in the best chance for success. We kendoka all know this because we've experienced it in our matches or training. We have all just let go, thrown ourselves into an attack, and somehow ended up triumphant. We can't really explain it, but nothing feels better than pulling off the ultimate no-mind (possibly mindless) sacrificial strike. Hence the disdain for blocking in kendo, and the importance attached to things like the never-say-die training method of *kakari-geiko*, or aiming to score the first point in the encounter (*shodachi*).

In any case, the teachings of the ancients really do serve to illuminate the present. There is a lot to be said for the wisdom to be gleaned from early-modern texts, which upon close inspection actually stacks up with cutting-edge 21st century sports psychology. Some wonderful translations are available for many of the classic books written by samurai in the early-modern period. See David Groff's excellent translation of Miyamoto Musashi's *Gorin-no-Sho*, for example. Even if you are only interested in kendo as a competitive sport rather than as a comprehensive "life philosophy", the psychosomatic knowledge that can be accessed in these old texts about bushido and the martial arts really do have a lot to offer the modern kendoka if you care to read between the lines. I found that my understanding of kendo helped me understand *Hagakure* at a deeper level, and my appreciation of *Hagakure* aided in my understanding of many kendo concepts in new, refreshing ways.

Miyako Tanaka Price (1942–2014)

Miyako was born in 1942 in Osaka, Japan, during the war years. Since Japanese cities were bombing targets, Miyako and her mother moved away from Osaka to her mother's native province. Her father went off to fight in the Philippines while her grandparents and great grandparents stayed in Osaka. American B-29s bombed the house she was born in but fortunately no one was hurt.

Japanese culture was a strong current in the Tanaka household. As a child Miyako helped her father in his sushi restaurant. Her father also taught *sadō* (tea ceremony) and *kadō* (flower arranging) in a teahouse in the family garden. Miyako held a teaching certificate in, and was a lifelong member of Urasenke, a school of tea centred in Kyoto.

Miyako's love of Japanese culture included naginata, a martial art practised primarily by women. Although all Japanese martial arts were banned during the Allied Occupation, naginata was allowed again in the 1950s and became a required physical education class for all female students at the university Miyako entered in 1961. In fact, naginata was the only physical education instruction offered to women enrolled at Kansai University.

Miyako's family was very liberal and encouraged her to study for professions few women considered at the time. Her grandfather wanted Miyako to be a medical doctor. Miyako's father instead wanted a lawyer in the family, so he encouraged Miyako to study for an MA in law, which she eventually attained. Miyako was one of the few female students at the university. At Kansai University there were only about 100 female students in her freshman class of 3,000 or 4,000. In the law department, out of about 800 students, only six or seven were women.

However, Miyako's heart was in naginata, not law. Although all female students had to study naginata, until then Kansai University was not producing many serious competitors at national competitions. In fact, no-one participated in the All Japan Naginata Federation national tournaments. Tokunaga Chiyoko was teaching naginata at the university and was instrumental in encouraging her students to compete. Tokunaga-sensei later would receive national and imperial awards for her work promoting this unique cultural art form, and is recognised as one of the founders of modern naginata. Tokunaga-sensei and Miyako developed a close relationship over the years. In her biography, Tokunaga-sensei, out of the countless students she taught, singles out Miyako's naginata skill and understanding as "marvelous". It is accurate to say that Miyako's knowledge of naginata was unsurpassed by anyone in her generation or since.

Miyako started the Kansai University Naginata Club in 1963, and she gave the introductory remarks at the 50th Anniversary celebration of the Club in Osaka in September 2013. In 1979, the Japanese Ministry of Education sent Miyako to Southern California to teach naginata for a year. There, Miyako met Steve Price through his friends Malyne and Alyne Hazard, both accomplished kendoka in California.

Miyako and Steve married in the backyard of his parents' house in Whittier, California, in 1984. Steve was living at the time in Oakland. Together they moved to El Cerrito, California. Miyako has taught both the modern and classical forms of naginata, *Atarashi Naginata* and Tendo-ryū Naginata-jutsu, at the El Cerrito Community Center since 1989. She co-founded the Northern California Naginata Federation in 1990 and served as President of the United States Naginata Federation for over a decade.

She occasionally taught in Canada, the Netherlands, Sweden, Brazil, and various dojo across the United States. As a direct result of her dedication and unparalleled skills as an instructor, Miyako's students have gone on to be national and international champions, teachers, and leaders in the naginata world.

In 2012, Miyako was awarded the highest rank in naginata—Hanshi—making her the highest-ranked practitioner outside of Japan, and one of less than 200 people to achieve the rank. She is survived by her husband, mother and two brothers in Osaka, and a host of loving students, friends and extended family.

By Kurt Schmucker, the current president of the U.S. Naginata Federation, and who was a student of Tanaka-sensei from the late 1980s. This article is adapted from the biography written by Steve Price, Tanaka-sensei's husband.

HANSHI SAYS

A series in which some of Japan's top Hanshi teachers give hints of what they are looking for in grading examinations based on wisdom accumulated through decades of training.

Translated by Alex Bennett - *Kendo World* would like to thank Taba-sensei and *Kendo Jidai* Magazine for permission to translate and publish this article.

Taba Norinobu *(Hanshi 8-dan)*

I look at how much the candidate is unsettling his opponent before striking.

Taba Norinobu-sensei was born in Okinawa in 1937. After graduating from Naha High School, he entered the police force in Okinawa, and became a member of the elite kendo squad. After serving as the Shihan for Okinawa Prefecture Police Kendo, Taba-sensei retired in 1996. Taba-sensei had an illustrious competitive career, and fought in all of the major tournaments in Japan, and placed third at the National 8-dan Championships held in Okinawa in 1999. He also served as the president of the Okinawa Kendo Federation. He passed the 8-dan examination in 1990, and was awarded Hanshi in 1998.

Are you able to fluster your opponent with *ki*, make an opportunity and then strike it?

When I am on an examination panel for 8-dan examinations, the main thing that I am looking for in my assessment is whether or not the candidate demonstrates an understanding of correct kendo theory. In other words, are they fighting their opponent from an interval that seems close to them but far away for the opponent? Are they seizing the right opportunities to strike? Are they attacking with *ki-ken-tai-itchi* (the unification of spirit, sword and body)? And, are they demonstrating steadfast *zanshin* at the end of each attack? The act of applying pressure is essentially a clash of two minds, and the key for success is how well each candidate is able take the initiative in the *seme* process of attack and defence. Strong "*ki-zeme*"—overcoming your opponent with your spirit and presence—is of the essence.

In other words, to take the initiative, first you need to have a strong presence which puts the opponent under pressure. If your application of pressure in this way is effective, you will be able to control the optimum distance, and your opponent will falter as a matter of course. This is when you create an opening (*tsukuri*) and a striking opportunity arises. You must be ready to seize it without fail. Regardless of whether or not the resulting strike is successful, the point is to be able to identify the opening and capitalise on it.

My teacher in the police, Sakuma Kenyū-sensei, always used to say, "Even though Okinawa is a long way from the mainland, as long as our *seme* is strong, our kendo will be recognized everywhere." His *seme* and spirit was so unforgiving, when we went up against him in training, we would quickly become flummoxed and unable to move freely. His "*ki-zeme*" was truly intense.

The other important aspect is "*tsukuri*", in which you draw your opponent into making a premature attack. Through a superior psychological presence, the opponent will panic and rush into making attacks. You can then ride his wave of insecurity and impatience, and pick him off at will with counterattacks.

You also need to have "*tame*" to be able to do this successfully. *Tame* is the feeling of being composed, patient, and replete in spirit, making each strike weighty and decisive. Having *tame* also means that you will not succumb to your opponent's *seme*, and that you are always brimming with vigour and ready to explode into action at exactly the right moment. If you can demonstrate this quality in your examination, the examiners will also feel your presence and put a tick next to your name. As the examiners are also highly-ranked kendoka, they are particularly sensitive to matters of *ki*, and can easily identify who is controlling the other.

In the course of my usual training, I often ask my students, "Did you see an opportunity to strike? Or, did you fall into my trap and feel compelled to attack?" This is something all practitioners must be able to answer themselves. Sakuma-sensei used to advise us not to strike against our will, and not to be cajoled into attacking. But still, we were always in the palm of his hands. It takes many years of training to be able to break free from the psychological clutches of a great teacher when fighting him; you have to be aware of how you are being controlled. Reflect on why this is so. Eventually you will be able to see how it happens to you, and how you can make it happen by exerting the same pressure on others.

Are you able to strike in a state of no-mind (*mushin*)?

There was a period of time when I attended an "image training" class where I learned how to turn negatives into positives. This helped me appreciate the idea that if I am struck in kendo, it is actually teaching me correct kendo principles and theory. Through this, each and every *ippon* in my kendo training took on more significance, and I felt a sense of gratitude to my opponents when I was able to hit them and vice versa. This really helped me to improve.

Image training is not just a matter of imagining your own ideal form and successful attacks. It requires contemplation of optimum striking opportunities. You imagine and identify openings in an opponent's movement, and go over them in your mind. Then, when engaging in *keiko*, use this imagery and strike at the same openings without concern for whether or not the attack is successful. More often than not you will end up failing. However, it will help you cultivate your powers of intuition, and will lead on to the ability to make an attack in a state of *mushin*. It will also help you appreciate the depth of kendo, and make training more fulfilling. If you lose to yourself (mentally), then you will inevitably be hit by your opponent. In other words, always wanting to strike, while constantly avoiding being struck will ultimately result in the latter.

In a hard fought bout, the ultimate objective is to polish your ability, and learn to strike with *mushin*. If you can enter a state of no-mind, your opponent's movements will become more apparent, and you will be able to take the initiative (*sen*). You will end up striking unconsciously, which is the ideal. This is what is meant by having increased powers of "intuition". Everybody has this ability deep down; it is just a matter of knowing how to tap it. This ability connects to *mushin*. I think that people have all but forgotten the importance of intuition.

Miyamoto Musashi writes of this in *Gorin-no-Sho*. The warrior needs to be able to see externally and internally (*kanken-no-metsuke*). However, he advises to pay more attention to seeing through the opponent rather than just the surface. This is intuition, but can only be realised through many years of rigorous training. Once you get it, you will know when you opponent is serious about making an attack, or is just trying to coax you into making a move.

Are you putting your back into your strikes?

Miyamoto Musashi wrote that examination, formulation, disciplining the body and mind, prudence and *keiko* are all crucial elements to excel in the martial arts. This indeed stands true for our study of kendo, and also provides a direction in life. For kendo to meet its oft-touted objective of "character development", it requires training with all of one's heart. Bouts with others is a crucial part of this, and it becomes quite evident how strong your heart really is in the fray. No matter how straight your posture is, and strong your *kamae* looks, the examiners will be able to see straight through you if there is nothing inside to back it up.

So, how do you infuse your kendo with heart? By putting your back into it. In other words, all of your striking should be done from the hips and lower back area, not just the hands. This kind of striking is requisite for people striving for higher ranks. Especially for 8-dan, elegance and poise is expected, and this is dictated by the back of your neck and back. If these are perfectly straight and upright, you will be able strike with your hips, and it will look powerful and beautiful.

Next, the position of your left hand is also important, especially when striking *men*. It should not be raised too high or too low as this will make the strike weak, and it will show that the hands and feet are not in sync. The right hand, right elbow and shoulder should be in a horizontal line. It looks good, and will show the examiners that the line of your cut and its strength are perfectly adequate. It also shows that you have spent many years practising kendo the correct way.

Even if the swing is small, as long as *tenouchi* is effectively applied, the strike will be crisp and decisive with "*sae*". This way, it will look much bigger than what the swing actually is, and the examiners will be impressed. There is no need to try and make all of your swings big when they do not need to be. To achieve this kind of *tenouchi*, be sure to do plenty of *suburi*, always keeping in mind the importance of *ki-ken-tai-itchi*.

Ultimately, examiners are human beings too, so if you keep working away at your kendo and trying to fix all of the minor details you are not happy with, the results of your efforts will eventually pay off. Strike at the heart, with the heart. That is what I continue working at in my keiko. If you can do this, then you will be successful at winning the hearts of the examiners.

EMBRACE THE FAILING

By Boris Jansen

I am still on a high after passing my kendo 6-dan in August 2013. The preparation, failing, reflection, struggling and finally passing the exam, turned out to be a much greater experience than I initially expected. The failing forced me to take a step back and helped me to transform my kendo into what I believe is more mature and varied, and on top of it, just more fun. In this article, I would like to share my experience regarding my three attempts and highlight some of the requirements that I think are key in order to pass.

It is often said that 6-dan is a big step up from 5-dan. In Japan, this is partly reflected by the fact that the 6-dan examinations are organised by the All Japan Kendo Federation, in contrast to the examinations up to 5-dan, which are conducted by the prefectural and city kendo federations. At each of the 6-dan exams conducted about seven times a year throughout Japan, more than 1000 candidates take part, with the exception of the yearly exam in Tokyo on the last Monday of November, where there are about 2000 candidates. The average pass rate is between 15% and 20%. For candidates who failed, there is an opportunity to fill out a postcard with your

address and exam number to receive feedback regarding your performance. On the postcard, the organisation will mark one out of three options:

A- You are very close to passing
B- You are to some extent on the right track
C- You are far from passing

For my first attempt in August 2012, I was full of confidence, as I had not experienced any difficulties up to 5-dan. Also, as a national team member for the Netherlands for the past 16 years, my focus had mostly been on *shiai* and I considered progressing on the ladder of *dan* grades as more or less a natural result of training hard at international level. For the practical component, *jitsugi*, I planned to suppress some of my *shiai* instincts, and set my main objectives to:

1—Strike with full spirit
2—Not strike too often; and
3—Keep a correct posture. These are all very similar to what I did for my 5-dan examination.

I followed through on my own objectives, but felt most strikes had not been convincing enough to be considered a full *ippon*. Therefore it was a disappointment, but not a surprise, to see I had failed the exam. However, by observing other candidates with a similar style or performance as my own, and their results, I also started to realise that even if I could have landed my strikes better, I probably still would have failed. Just making accurate strikes, *yūkō-datotsu*, with correct posture did not seem sufficient. The postcard in my mailbox one week later also informed me I got a "C"—basically, none of the examiners thought I should have passed.

In many of the candidates who I did see pass, I observed two characteristics that I think made their kendo stand out and contributed significantly to their success. First of all, their *jitsugi* was truly full of spirit. I had set a "full spirit" goal myself, but I had limited it only to my strikes. These candidates demonstrated full spirit from beginning to end, not only in their strikes, but also in their *kamae*, *seme*, *zanshin*, even in their *rei* and *sonkyo*. Part of this spirit was simply expressed in loud *kiai*, but it was expressed in their *seme* through taking the initiative throughout the *tachiai*, and in the absence of hesitation in their attacks.

There were other candidates who also showed full spirit, but still failed the exam. I think many of those candidates often lacked the second characteristic, which perhaps can be best labelled as *kigurai*. The successful candidates displayed confidence and elegance. It was not arrogance, or the result of ignorance, which enabled the former group to strike without hesitation. Rather, this was a kind of confidence powered by understanding and determination.

Back in the dojo, I started to feel lost. I knew I had quite some work to do in order to pass 6-dan, but I did not really understand yet what I had to do. I worked on "spirit" and tried to increase the impact of my strikes by giving more *kiai* and making my swings bigger; as a result, my kendo became quite static and more often than not my techniques were counterattacked by my opponents. What started to puzzle me even more was wondering how could I land a couple of good *ippon* on a candidate who is also testing for his 6-dan in only a minute or so? Many *shiai* take the full five minutes and often none or only one *ippon* is decided. How does one score multiple clean *ippon*, unforced, in a short amount of time? This thought started to unnerve me.

My second attempt was too soon after the first with only three months in between. I had improved one thing though. My strikes were full of spirit and had a bigger impact, but overall the changes were mainly physical. One sensei with access to the exam data told me I was one vote short of passing, confirmed later by the postcard with the "A" marked. The main difference between the first try and the second was that I was not trying to put on a show anymore, but fought for each *ippon* from start to finish. Still, I was not content at all with my performance, even though it seemed I was getting closer to passing. I lacked confidence, and felt I had not made any significant progress yet.

In one *keiko* with Toyomura-sensei, one of the two 8-dan sensei in my dojo, I reached the peak of my frustrations. He was playing with me as if I had just started kendo, and the harder I tried the worse it got. After practice, he told me that what was hindering my development was that I did not want to get hit. He advised me to slightly raise my left hand in *kamae*, open up, and to develop a mindset of inviting your opponent to attack. Do not care about getting hit, only care about putting your own full spirit in every action.

This was not the first time that something along these lines had been said to me, but perhaps because of the frustrations and my struggling, I was more willing to really try and follow this advice. By doing so, things started to improve rather quickly. By not caring about getting hit, I ironically got hit less. By inviting the opponent, rather than constantly searching for an opening to attack, I not only improved my *ōji-waza*, but I also discovered more opportunities to attack when the opponent would not respond to my *seme*. By slightly raising my left hand and focusing on keeping a correct and straight posture, my striking distance became slightly closer and as a result my strikes naturally gained in impact. By overcoming the fear of getting hit, I felt my kendo started to improve on many fronts.

On my third attempt in August 2013, nine months after my second, my confidence was back. It was a different kind of confidence though, compared to my first try. Regardless of the outcome of the exam, I was very satisfied with the changes my kendo had undergone. I sensed that my kendo had matured significantly. Now I only needed to show this to the grading panel.

My first opponent had demonstrated strong kendo in the *jitsugi* before me, and I thought he was well on track to pass. We rose from *sonkyo* and pressured each other, fighting for the centre. Finally, I felt I was on top and he was not able to strike anymore.

I jumped, but my first attack, *men*, got countered by a strong *kaeshi-dō*. I thought after this the examiners would not let me pass, but I pushed that thought out of my mind immediately. I strongly suppressed the urge to try to make up for it quickly, knowing that the *tachiai* would only last only about 10 seconds more. The remainder felt good though, as if I had come back from an *ippon* behind in a hard fought *shiai*. The second *jitsugi* went very well, and I scored *men*, *debana-kote* and *kaeshi-dō* on my opponent, whom I felt resembled the state I was in during my first 6-dan attempt.

This was by far my best attempt. The only reason I thought they could fail me is because of the first *kaeshi-dō* countering my *men*. Anyway, I was confident that I could now pass 6-dan with my current kendo. When the numbers of the candidates who passed the *jitsugi* appeared, I saw the number of my first opponent. It took me another moment to realise that my number was next on the list—I had passed.

As mentioned above, many consider 6-dan a big step up from 5-dan. I think the reason for this is that the importance assigned to the different requirements on which candidates are evaluated changes significantly from 5-dan to 6-dan. I believe that 5-dan is a continuation of 4-dan, with very similar requirements, although at a higher level. The majority of the assessment for candidates trying for 5-dan is still done at the technical-skill level. In short, the candidates are required to demonstrate that they have mastered and refined a wide range of techniques, and have a good understanding of *maai* and correct application of *seme*.

While technical skills of course remain an important aspect, I think for 6-dan the focus shifts from the evaluation of technical skills to the appraisal of the candidate's mental state. First of all, the candidate is required to display an understanding of what defines and results in a valid strike. Any strike needs to be the result of well executed *seme*. I believe you will get a higher evaluation if you truly pressure your opponent with full spirit and strike at the right time, even if you miss the target, compared to strikes that connect but are short on *seme*. For example, strikes based on power or speed, or just waiting for the opponent to attack in order to apply *ōji-waza*. It takes confidence and courage to fight for each *ippon* by applying *seme* and have tension build up, but I believe this is vital in order to pass 6-dan. It was my initial mistake to treat the 6-dan exam as an advanced 5-dan exam.

I often think about what would have happened if I had passed the first or second time. I wonder if I would have been able to achieve similar growth in my kendo, and if so, when, if I had to do it without this strong drive to pass the exam? Therefore, I am grateful to the sensei who failed me the first time, and even more so the second. Although I feel I have made great progress, so many new doors have been opened that it also feels as though I am just at the beginning of a wonderful new journey, and for the first time I am eagerly looking forward to the challenges the next exam may bring. For anybody who is currently struggling with an exam, or may do in the future, I would like to say, "embrace the failing". Take a step back and enjoy it. It may be one of the best times in your kendo life.

Grading Successfully: Part 2

By Shigematsu Kimiaki, Kendo K8-dan
Translated by Remi Yamaguchi

"Cultivating your own kendo philosophy"

People "play" in the world of sports, but in the Japanese arts the act of training is known as "*keiko*". The literal meaning of "*keiko*" is to "ponder ancient ways" or "study ancient things". In other words, it means to study the teachings of our predecessors, and emphasises the importance of our mental attitude towards the arts. As practitioners of kendo, we need to be aware of our responsibility to preserve this valuable culture, and pass it on to future generations in the correct way. By reconsidering the meaning of *keiko*, and training ourselves accordingly, I believe that we will be able to develop an even more vibrant and relevant kendo philosophy.

1. *Kirikaeshi* and *uchikomi* help you foster real strength

Kirikaeshi and *uchikomi* are important types of *keiko* that will help to solidify the foundations of your kendo. Since it is hard for regular people to secure enough time to practise due to work or family commitments, most end up doing mainly *ji-geiko* (*gokaku-geiko*) and not so much *kirikaeshi*. However, you need to make an effort to find time to do *kirikaeshi* and *uchikomi*.

Ideal *kirikaeshi* is described as being "big, strong, quick, and light". When a beginner does *kirikaeshi*, it needs to be executed in a big, correct motion, and then becomes gradually stronger. As you become better trained, it becomes quicker, and eventually light and graceful.

Kirikaeshi is a combination of *shōmen* and *sayū men* strikes, and is a method of *keiko* that allows you to comprehensively attain basic movements. Often, I see kendo practitioners mistakenly strike *shōmen*, then take four steps forward and five back while striking, and then finish at that point. That is the basic method of *kirikaeshi* for instructing beginners. Originally, it was not decided how many strikes would be made; instead the attacker would follow the *motodachi*'s lead, and strike however many times, and then finish on the *motodachi*'s signal.

Uchikomi-geiko is where the *motodachi* intentionally creates an opening or an opportunity for a strike so that the attacker can take advantage of it. Since *uchikomi-geiko* is driven by the *motodachi*, it is important that the level of the practitioner is determined to allow them to get the best out of each practice. In *uchikomi-geiko*, it is crucial that each and every strike meets the requirements for *yūkō-datotsu*. You need to constantly keep posture, spirit, *maai*, sharpness of *tenouchi*, footwork, breath control, etc., in mind and strike so that each one counts. It is easy to say that each strike should be a *yūkō-datotsu* (valid strike), but in actuality it is very difficult to achieve.

When I was a *tokuren* member in the police, I had the opportunity to visit various places for *keiko* and receive valuable instruction from many different sensei. Back then, all *keiko* ended with *uchikomi* or *kakari-geiko*, and *kirikaeshi*. Even if the sensei did not say "*ippon*", we would have said "Thank you very much" when struck, and asked for *uchikomi* and *kirikaeshi*. If the content and quality of our *keiko* was poor, *uchikomi* and *kirikaeshi* would last forever. After *keiko*, we would be completely out of breath, panting for air, and would have absolutely no energy left. However, this is the kind of *keiko* that helps you gain real strength. At that time I thought it was unbearable, but now I am truly grateful to have received it.

These days, there are not too many people who ask for *uchikomi* and *kirikaeshi* willingly after *keiko*, which is a real shame. I wonder if not many people understand the importance of *uchikomi* and *kirikaeshi*. Doing *ji-geiko* alone will not help you gain real strength. *Uchikomi* and *kirikaeshi* are hard, but that is the very reason why it offers you gains afterwards. I imagine most people honestly want to avoid it, but I am convinced that by doing *uchikomi* and *kirikaeshi* you can gain real strength, even if your practice time may be short.

In the end, basic training is the quickest way to improve. There is a teaching that goes, "By learning the basics, you will create a foundation to apply the basics to. To reach a higher-level of application, you need to learn the basics even more thoroughly." So, if you are at a loss as to what to do, go back to basics.

2. "Two-faced" *keiko*

The only way to pass a grading examination is to train yourself. To do this, you need to plan how much time to spend on what, and execute that plan well so that you can build your basic strength. Sometimes you will not pass the exam, even though you have what it takes. Sometimes, you will not be able to fully demonstrate your ability, or perhaps you keep failing despite your ability. One of the possible reasons could be that the content of your training is far from what the actual grading exam is like.

Specifically, you should refrain from doing "two-faced" *keiko*. In other words, you should always give your best regardless of the situation. Anybody will do their very best when doing *keiko* with their sensei. However, there are many people who relax too much when practising with people who are either of the same grade or lower than themselves. They are forgetting what their sensei said during *shidō-geiko* and are just repeating their flawed *keiko* routine. In Japanese, this is known as "*hoi hoi kendō*" (thoughtless kendo); it lacks seriousness. People that practise like this will not pass a grading, and even if they were fortunate enough to pass, I doubt that their grade would represent their true ability. They will then be guaranteed to experience extreme hardships at later gradings.

No matter who you are training with, or what their grade is, you should strictly follow the advice you receive from your sensei. This is what makes your kendo better. It is probably difficult for you to break your sensei's composure with your *seme* to score a *yūkō-datotsu*. If you face those of the same or lower grade with the same kind of passion, however, you should be able to land a strike that everybody, including the person struck, will be in awe of.

There is no *keiko* better than that done with *aiki*, where both practitioners are fully committed and giving 100%. No matter how short the *keiko* is, it is always meaningful. *Keiko* that lacks seriousness is a complete waste of time, and people will not think highly of you. There is no *keiko* uglier than when the two practitioners do not have *aiki*.

You are required to score *yūkō-datotsu* in a limited time during grading exams, something that is extremely difficult to achieve. The judges do not have time to watch you for five minutes, let alone ten, so in your daily *keiko*, you always need to aim to get a *yūkō-datotsu* in a short amount of time. In the exam, you will not be able to do what you normally do not do during *keiko*. Therefore, even though it is difficult, in your everyday *keiko*, try to do the best you can in a short amount of time.

3. The right attitude

(1) *Keiko* with people of a higher level

When doing *keiko* with higher level sensei, it is important to feel grateful that you are receiving *shidō-geiko*. At the same time, you need to "feel equal" at the time of the *shodachi* (first cut) and aim for an *ippon*. In other words, you need to think of *keiko* as an *ippon-shōbu*. After the *shodachi*, you need to be the one to attack, and you cannot back down or avoid cuts – you should always give 100%.

To be the "one to attack" means that you should avoid doing deceitful or cunning kendo, and instead face your opponent head on. Also, if you are too focused on hitting your opponent, and too busy contemplating how to do it, that means that your mind is not clear. *Keiko* like this is meaningless. Furthermore, trying to avoid your sensei's cut, or doing *keiko* as if at the same level, is out of the question.

Unfortunately, I feel that the training menu for *shidō-geiko* these days is different from that of my youth. It is often impossible to tell the difference between the *motodachi* and *kakarite*. This is the kind of *keiko* where the *kakarite* merely waits for the *motodachi* sensei to attack and then tries to scrape their *kote*. When watching such *keiko*, you cannot see the *kakarite*'s determination to give it their all. Perhaps they are not very grateful about receiving *keiko*. It is crucial to not wait, but to attack with total commitment; after *keiko* you should be so drained that you have nothing left. This is the kind of *keiko* that improves your kendo. Make sure to have a short *keiko* that is rich in content – the kind that leaves you out of breath.

(2) *Keiko* with people of the same level

Doing *keiko* with people of the same level (*gokaku-geiko*) is just as important as that with high level sensei. Since people of the same level and a similar age are matched against each other during gradings, doing *keiko* with them helps you to determine your capabilities, and is therefore very important. It is like a mock exam, so you need to pay attention to your posture, *seme*, strikes, *zanshin* and taking *yūkō-datotsu*. It is a perfect opportunity to see if you can remain patient, whether your *waza* is good enough, and so on. If you find yourself content with the result, it means that you are one step closer to the *dan* you want to achieve.

Despite their aspirations, however, when doing *gokaku-geiko*, some people do it in the wrong way simply because they want to strike but do not want to be struck. If you get struck, it means your opponent has found a weakness, and you should be grateful for the lesson. Do *keiko* with humility and gratitude.

(3) *Keiko* with people of a lower level

There are two types of *keiko* with people of a lower level: one where you try to improve your skills; the other where you try to improve your opponent's.

First, how can you use this type of *keiko* to your advantage and improve your own skills? The answer is simple: do not relax. You still need *aiki* and to be equally committed. There are, however, some people who do not do their best when facing lower level opponents. This is meaningless *keiko* which only satisfies people's hunger for seemingly scoring with ease.

Having *keiko* with lower-level people is extremely important to physically learn *riai* – the principles behind the techniques. It is also a perfect opportunity to study *seme* as well as improve your striking skills. Make sure you engage in *keiko* with the understanding that it is the best chance to learn opportunities for strikes. In other words, reassure yourself that it is an opportunity to learn how to put theory into practice with your techniques.

Second, this type of *keiko* also augments the ability of the lower level practitioner. Known as "*hikitate-geiko*", it teaches the *kakarite* the joy of making a successful strike, as well as the right timing for strikes. *Kakarite* usually do *keiko* with a certain goal in mind, such as passing a grading. This means the role that *motodachi* plays in guiding the lower ranks is even more important. During *hikitate-geiko*, make them feel the severity of *seme*, and what a solid strike is. This experience will help them improve tremendously later on.

In kendo *keiko*, both you and your opponent are like a whetstone, using each other to polish your own technique and mind. When you are *motodachi*, it goes without saying that training the *kakarite* to improve their skills is important. At the same time, you need to train them mentally. When you are leading *shidō-geiko*, make *kakarite* think, "I'm so glad I asked him/her to train me. I would love to ask him/her to train me again." The last thing you want is to have them think, "I would never want to train with that SOB again." Therefore, be careful not to offer an uninspiring training session.

It is essential to engage in *keiko* with the understanding that both you and your opponent will apply pressure on each other, and try to break each other's composure. It is vital to polish your "sense of intuition", or "*kizashi*". Opportunities arising from *kizashi* are not something that can be seen with the eyes, but are felt in the mind, emanating from a slight difference in *ki*. The best part of kendo is to attack each other while feeling *kizashi*. If you merely strike each other with a *shinai* aimlessly, you will never be able to improve your sensitivity to the fluctuations in *ki*.

4. Forging *ki*

Every kendo practitioner has a "wall of *ki*", but that wall is thin and fragile without enough training. The more training you have, and the more experience you gain, the thicker and stronger the wall becomes. When doing *keiko* with a *kōdansha* (a person with a high *dan* grade) you will often find yourself unable to strike no matter how hard you try. Their invisible wall closes in on you, suffocates and leaves you unable to move, and you end up getting struck instead.

It is easy to understand the striking opportunities that judges and *kōdansha* prefer are the ones where the *ki* of the striker is strong. Cuts made during striking opportunities revealed through the offence and defence of *ki* are regarded highly; strikes made merely with speed are considered as "hitting" without intent or feeling, and are not given much credence.

An effective way to train your wall of *ki* and make it stronger is to release it against an experienced practitioner. If you discharge your *ki*, then the same or higher level of *ki* will bounce back at you. When you reach your limit, this will allow your *ki* to grow, and it will, slowly but surely, make your wall of *ki* thicker and stronger.

When attacking a high level sensei, even if you feel pressured by their *ki*, and even if you know that you are bound to get struck and your attacks countered, you still must confront your sensei so that you can forge your *ki*.

Sensei will tell you to train with people much stronger than you, and to attack them without hesitation. This is because they understand that the best way to improve in kendo is to forge *ki* through hard work.

Gokaku-geiko and *keiko* with people less skilled may help you improve your technique with the *shinai* and other skills, but it has little effect in building your *ki*. If you want to improve your kendo, you need to remember that attacking higher-level people is the only way to go.

5. Consider "*kyojitsu*"

"*Kyo*" (emptiness, unpreparedness) means weakness and an opening, and "*jitsu*" (being replete with *ki*, preparedness) is a strong point. In kendo, you aim to strike your opponent when an opening arises. You should not strike at *jitsu*. Create an opening if there is none. Look for, and capitalise on *kyo*. There are three kinds of openings: in mind; in posture; in movement. These openings are not separate entities, but are closely related. How you create an opening through offence and defence is an important element to the quality of the *yūkō-datotsu*.

While it is indeed important to find an opening in your opponent, what matters is the process of doing so.

There are no *kenshi* who show their openings (*kyo*). To elaborate, "*jitsu*" (one's strength) is shown externally, and "*kyo*" (weakness) is hidden underneath. To find a hidden opening, you need to break through the wall of your opponent's "*jitsu*". Your determination to break through is called "*sen*" (taking the initiative) and "*seme*" (applying pressure). A beginner's wall of *jitsu* is thin and easy to break, but when it comes to trained experts, their *jitsu* is stronger and harder to overcome.

No matter how many times you get repelled by the thick, strong wall of your opponent, you need to have strong belief and determination that you can break through, even by a millimetre. By continually doing *keiko* with such determination, it should give you something to build on in the future. As a result, this determination becomes the strength behind your *seme*. If you understand this, you will inevitably figure out what kind of *keiko* you need to do.

H9-dan Narazaki Masahiko-sensei said, "In kendo, it is important to find an opening to strike based on *kyojitsu*, but sometimes you need to have enough spirit so that you can face your opponent's *jitsu* with your own *jitsu*, and strike." Whether doing *keiko* with those who are of the same, higher, or lower level than you, doing it with the notion of *kyojitsu* in mind will make a difference in your progress. It may not bear fruit immediately, but you will reap the rewards in the future.

When I see the *keiko* of current junior high and high school students, they show almost no inkling that they are challenging their opponent. They seem more interested in picking up their opponent's openings for a lucky strike, rather than breaking their wall to get them to lower their guard. This is passive, opportunistic kendo. They start by defending themselves, and continue the rest of the match that way. The reason why they have ended up being like this, I think, has a lot to do with the way they are being taught. It is critical, in this sense, to reconsider the true nature of kendo.

6. Is your kendo good enough to match your *dan*?

As you need to express yourself during gradings, everybody becomes quite frantic. During exams, judges will evaluate your kendo and pass you if you meet the criteria as stated in Article 14 of the "*Regulations for Dan/Kyu and Shogo Title Certificates*" by the All Japan Kendo Federation. It is hard to pass a grading, but it is even more difficult to do kendo that matches the grade you received. There is nothing harder than this. Who do you think is judging your grade and your ability? Nobody engages in *keiko* announcing that he/she holds a certain *dan*. Those who assess your *dan* based on your true ability are your opponents in *keiko*, those who are waiting to train with you, and those who are watching your *keiko*. You need to do *keiko* that makes them say, "Of course he/she is X-*dan*." No matter what happens, your *keiko* must not make them say, "Blimey, does he/she really hold X-*dan*?"

The criteria for conferring *dan* and *kyū* grades are stated in Article 14 mentioned above. I wonder if anybody has ever thought about the criteria before. In addition, Article 16 states how many years of training are required before you can attempt the next grade. Why are there such requirements? From my understanding, it signifies a new task for your training after passing each grade, and that you need to use the years wisely and train so that you will be able to meet the criteria for the next level.

Therefore, it is advisable to establish concrete goals and improve your ability to be good enough to hold the conferred grade. For example, if the grade you earned is 5-dan, you should improve your ability so that you deserve 5.1-dan, 5.2-dan, 5.3-dan, etc., and as time passes, you should gradually go all the way up to 5.9-dan. This kind of effort will manifest itself as an apparent difference in ability between you and people of the same age and level.

In the next issue of KW, I will finish this series of articles with some advice about the attitude you should maintain in your everyday life to improve your kendo, and also the responsibilities you need to be aware of as you become higher in rank.

FIK ANTI-DOPING COMPLIANCE

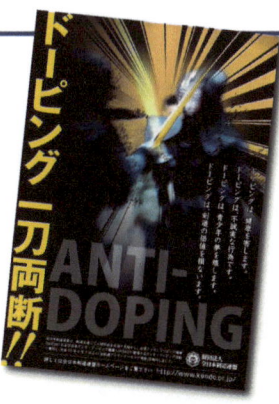

As an official member of SportAccord (formerly known as GAISF) the International Kendo Federation (FIK) set up an anti-doping committee to conform to the World Anti-Doping Agency (WADA) regulations pertaining to doping. As FIK affiliates, each national federation and participants in FIK activities must abide by the FIK Anti-Doping Rules compiled in accordance with the World Anti-Doping Code. Anybody found to be in violation of the Code will be subjected to severe sanctions, including ban from participation in future kendo events.

Dr. Darryl Tong (KW): Dr. Masayuki Miyasaka, in your capacity as the Chairman of the FIK Anti-Doping Committee, I would like to ask you about the FIK anti-doping policies and procedures. It seems that many national kendo federations around the world are new to the requirements, but are starting to understand it is now necessary to proactively deal with this problem. I would like to ask you to clarify a few points for KW readers.
First, what are the minimum requirements for a national federation to maintain an anti-doping policy?

Dr. Miyasaka: If your federation is affiliated to the FIK, and as FIK has accepted the WADA Code already, your federation needs to follow the FIK's anti-doping policy. Please read the FIK Anti-Doping Rules 2009 and also the FIK's anti-doping booklet, which are both downloadable from the FIK website (https://www.kendo-fik.org/). Additionally, you should consult your national anti-doping organization about this matter, as you may fall under its jurisdiction in the case that your federation belongs to the Olympic committee of your country.

KW: What are the required tests that the FIK wants to see done? E.g. random urine samples, blood screens?

Dr. Miyasaka: Once again, we advise you to consult your national anti-doping organisation about this matter. As the FIK, we perform in-competition tests at the WKC, whereas WADA performs out-of-competition tests for the FIK. Only those who belong to the Registered Testing Pool (RTP) receive this test; currently 12 FIK athletes are registered in the pool.

In the case of the All Japan Kendo Federation, we have in-competition tests at certain national-level competitions, and our national anti-doping organization (JADA) performs out-of-competition tests for RTP athletes. In all these tests, only urine samples have been tested, but WADA may start blood testing soon.

The RTP is comprised of athletes who are required to provide up-to-date information on their whereabouts to their organisation. This information is shared with WADA and other anti-doping organisations for the purposes of anti-doping testing, which may be conducted at any time.

KW: What is the expectation of frequency of testing? Random tests every six months, yearly or just prior to a major competition?

Dr. Miyasaka: We do not provide any fixed numbers for tests to be conducted by your federation. Again, you should consult your national anti-doping organization about this matter.

KW: Is there a standard template or format for reporting?

Dr. Miyasaka: Currently, we have no particular format for reporting.

KW: Will there be an audit from the FIK?
Dr. Miyasaka: No, we will make inquiries only in writing. As long as you follow WADA's guidelines, you should be compliant with FIK rules, or it can be the other way around, i.e., as long as you follow the FIK rules, you should be compliant with WADA's rules. If your federation is planning to create a document outlining policy and procedures within WADA/FIK guidelines, your national anti-doping organisation may have a pre-existing format which you could modify depending on your situation. It is best to contact them and seek advice.

KW: Most people who do kendo are amateurs. There is no prize money or commercial endorsements in kendo like other sports. Most people have no idea whatsoever what substances are prohibited. Does that mean that "as the stakes are lower" there will be more leniency shown to those who fail tests?

Dr. Miyasaka: No.

KW: Dr. Miyasaka, thank you very much for clarifying these issues.

For smaller national kendo federations, the cost of screening competitors at championships or national team members will most likely be extremely cost prohibitive. The least a federation can do as the international kendo community gets used to these requirements is to educate federation and squad members thoroughly in the dangers of doping, and what to look out for. This is the most efficient and effective way of preventing potential problems. All competitors need to be aware of doping guidelines, and the possibility of being tested at major competitions. Education is key. A good place to start is at the WADA homepage: http://www.wada-ama.org/

THE NUTS 'N' BOLTS OF KENDO

By Nakano Yasoji, (Kendo Hanshi 9-dan)   Translated by Alex Bennett

ALL ABOUT SHIAI

How should the relationship between *shiai* and *keiko* be thought of in kendo?

I think of *keiko* as a kind of *shiai*. *Kakari-geiko* is different, but in *ji-geiko* you should always aim to score the first point (*shodachi*). Even if you are doing *keiko* against your senpai or sensei, always try to get the first successful strike in, just as you would in a *shiai*. If you engage in *keiko* with this mindset but get hit instead, accept it with humility and say, "*mairimashita*" (I concede). If you manage to score a few good points against your sensei, and are satisfied, then it is time go all out and start *kakari-geiko*.

Attempting to get that first point is *keiko*'s connection with *shiai*. *Keiko* is different in that there is no *shinpan* involved, but is a very important opportunity to test a few techniques and try out their effectiveness.

There are some people who are very strong in *keiko*, but not so in *shiai*. Or, strong in *shiai*, but weak in *keiko*. How can this be so if *shiai* should be thought of as an extension of *keiko*?

When you say "strong" in *keiko*, exactly what strength are you referring to? Strong in terms of stamina or determination? This all has an influence in some way, but does not necessarily mean the full package.

In the old days, kendo matches were *juppon-shōbu* (ten points) or *gohon-shōbu* (five points), not *sanbon-shōbu* (three points) like today. All you have to do now is take two points, and you win the match. In *juppon-shōbu*, you had to engage in ten matches. In *gohon-shōbu* you had five matches, and if you won three, then you won overall. Fighting in ten bouts required incredible strength of will and skill to prevail. The true level of aggregate "strength" would be revealed eventually, one way or the other.

This is not the case anymore, and often the result is decided by luck–a few lucky hits, rather than by comprehensive strength and skill. Therefore, it is essential for kendoka to understand that winning a *sanbon-shōbu* match is not necessarily a true indication of actual personal skill or strength. Kendoka really should mull carefully about their mindset, posture, attitude, the way of creating openings, and so on. In other words, cumulative strength is the only real strength, not results from sporadic engagements. Furthermore, practitioners must study *shiai* through their regular *keiko*. Genuinely strong practitioners can defeat opponents in *shiai* as a matter of course with the techniques that they always use in *keiko*. They are one and the same.

What is the weight of psychological readiness compared to technical matters for success in *shiai*?

Of course, mental or psychological strength is vital in *shiai*, but first and foremost, mastering the techniques is the priority. After all, kendo matches are decided through an exchange of techniques with the opponent. Everybody needs techniques up their sleeve that can be used to overcome certain kinds of opponents. It is not a matter of deciding to use a particular *waza* before the match begins; it is largely dependent on the opponent's style. You need enough in your repertoire to deal with various situations.

To be able to do this, you must have solid fundamentals and be able to adapt as the situation requires. If you have researched various *waza* carefully, have made them your own, and are able to execute an appropriate *waza* for any given situation, then this is truly a high level of kendo.

Conversely, if you only have a limited number of techniques, then your kendo will be ineffectual if your opponent is able to read them. If one thing does not work, then you need to have another option, and then another on top of that. *Waza* should be considered from various angles, and be able to be applied in various circumstances. This is easier said than done, of course, and only a true master is able to execute various *waza* at the most opportune times, in accordance with the kind of opponent he or she is facing at that moment. I, too, still have a long way to go…

So, constantly repeating the basics is mandatory for reaching this level. That way, when you are engaged in a match, you will be able to adapt without even thinking about it. But, you must have the basics well and truly mastered first, and be able to read the situation to decide what technique will work best.

Lots of people get nervous when they participate in matches. It is not so easy to keep calm in such a situation, but what do you recommend as the best way to keep your nervousness in check?

It is true, many people cannot perform to their best ability because of their nerves. In the pressure environment of a tournament, competitors gradually manage to calm down after the second or third round, but the first is tricky in terms of overcoming anxiety. Personally, when I am nervous at a *shiai*, I think of some kind of old motto to take my mind off things and get focused. For example,

Noma Hisashi wrote in his book *Kendō Tokuhon* that he calms down by thinking, "I am the best in Japan". In my case, before a match, I read a passage from one of my favorite books, such as *Tengū Geijutsu-ron*. When I have finished my first fight, I refuse to observe any other matches going on. I will take a peek at who I will be fighting in the second round, but that is all.

But just calming the mind down is not enough. The body also tends to be stiff from nerves. So, I do *suburi* making sure that each swing counts. I do three sets of ten. I also sit in *seiza* and concentrate on my breathing. I breathe in deeply for a count of five, and then exhale slowly for a count of 15. I do this three times. This makes me relaxed and focused. I do not get as nervous as I used to in my younger days, but I still go through this routine, as I find it helps.

In any case, it is better not to watch the other matches if you can, unless he or she is going to be your next opponent, or it is somebody you are close to. Watching

kendo matches drains you of energy, and also makes you more tense. If you watch randomly here and there, you will lose concentration, and your energy will wane.

Even if you have trained hard to embody the fundamental techniques, how do you know the best time to employ them during the match?
This is difficult. Even if you have a good level of proficiency in the basics, it is easy to tense up at the critical moment. That is why in addition to techniques, you need to cultivate your mettle and pluck. Without strong willpower, your techniques will never work, no matter how well you may have mastered the basic forms.

The next thing is to know your opponent. For example, in my younger days I participated in a match between Japan and Manchuria in 1941. My opponent was a guy called Kanazawa who was originally from Ibaraki prefecture. Just before the match, I spotted him taking *kamae*. His *kensen* was slightly to the right, so I knew straight away that he was most likely going to be very good at suckering his opponents into attacking, and then finishing them off with *kaeshi-waza* or the like. This meant that at some stage he would probably lift his hands up leaving *kote* or *dō* open.

When the match started, I consciously assailed him with *seme* from the *omote* side, and just as he sensed I was going to attack, he lifted his hands slightly to receive, and I so struck his *kote*. The same thing happened, and I struck his *dō*. I was able to beat him by two points by reading his idiosyncrasies based on his *kamae*, and by knowing how to deal with an opponent with his style.

This is a very important part of *keiko*. Always try to identify styles, and research the best kind of techniques to use for different opponents. This will bolster your confidence, and will help stop you becoming too nervous.

A similar story still fresh in my memory was my match against Kojima-sensei (H9-dan) at the Kyoto Taikai. His style of kendo was quite traditional, and not of the frenetic variety. He usually applied *seme* from below, and then struck *kote* as his opponent reacted. His *kamae* was quite low. I went over the top of his *shinai* and struck his inside *kote* from above. It made quite a noise on contact. For the next point, I let go with a thrust to his throat just as he tried to move forward. Learning from my father-in-law (Mochida Moriji), I made sure that my back was firmly activated in the thrust, and I turned my left hand inwards just before the tip of my *shinai* connected. This allows a little more range. As he was reacting by moving in to take the thrust with the intention of letting it slide off, I was able to pull the *kensen* back slightly because I had given myself enough room, and finished him off with a decisive *men* strike.

In any case, the point is to be able to identify your opponent's weakness or habits, and be able to take advantage of them with rational, appropriate *waza* selection. If you can do this, then you will be a great kendoka. This is what you should aspire to, but it requires a bit of preparation and forethought, and proactive experimentation during training.

What are some of the things you can use as hints to identify your opponent's style of kendo?

As I have just said, it is easier to manage your opponent if you know his or her habits. If you do not, however, you should keep your distance at first, and observe the way they try to attack you. If they do not come after you, then take the initiative and start applying more pressure, and then strike their *kote* or the like when they are forced to react. This is one pattern. My father used to suddenly lower his *kensen* slightly, not with the intention of making a strike, but to conjure a movement in the opponent and to see how they reacted.

A very important clue can be found in the opponent's *kamae*. Look at the height of their *kensen*, the direction it is pointing in, and foot positioning, etc. Ogawa-sensei had a perfectly straight *kamae*, and used to approach very swiftly. His techniques were very orthodox. Nakakura-sensei, on the other hand, would approach as he shouldered his *shinai*, and unleash all manner of techniques often flustering his opponents. You must be prepared mentally if you are facing an opponent who has a huge repertoire of *waza*, and not let yourself be overcome from the outset. Similarly, when engaging in *keiko* with university students or the like, of course they are going to be extremely fast and tricky, so the secret is to not spend too much time contemplating the situation, and do not give them time to attack. If you steal their thunder, openings for you to strike will appear.

Having said that, it is still hard to read an experienced kendo practitioner. Young kendoka may be fast, but they do not have much weight in their strikes. A more mature kendoka is slower, but there is more intent in each move, and therefore their attacks end up being more dangerous. Take this into consideration as well.

Do external influences such as the venue effect your performance in any way?

Actually, I have a funny story about venues. The 1st Inter-Prefectural Tournament was held in Miyazaki Prefecture. The final for the individual and the team events were held outside on a stage that was set up in a baseball diamond. I was in the final for the individuals, and just as the match started, the sun came out. It was very hard to see, so I manoeuvred to the left forcing my opponent to face the bright rays of sunshine. Obviously, this put him at a disadvantage, and I ended up striking his *dō* as he felt compelled to strike. I do not feel bad about this as it is all a part of strategy. You have to use what is at hand to your benefit, otherwise it will be used against you.

What about when you have to fight untraditional matches such as against a *naginata* or *nitō* player?

I actually find fighting against *nitō* easier than *jōdan*. All you have to do is kill their *shōtō* (short sword). A *nitō* player will try to suppress your *shinai* with the *shōtō* first, before following up with an attack. Make them lift their *shōtō* up and then strike them, or use *suriage-waza* against their attacks. They will have a hard time landing a successful strike.

Also, *nitō* players generally block attacks against their *men* with the *shōtō*, and then follow up straight away with an attack with their *daitō*. So, just as they are about to block your *men* strike, immediately change direction and strike *gyaku-dō* instead. You will be too late if you look for the opening first. Strike with that intention from the outset, knowing that they will try and block with the *shōtō*. If you apply pressure, they will most certainly try and defend. Just remember, do not let them use their *shōtō* to defend, and do not be mesmerized by their *daitō*.

As far as *naginata* is concerned, it is just a matter of getting experience and becoming used to the fact that they will strike at your legs (*sune*). Takano Sasaburō-sensei was an expert at lifting his front leg up and then following up with a *men* strike, or striking them as they were moving back. Once you have taken the element of surprise away, *naginata* or *nitō* are not so hard to beat.

In all of these scenarios, the message is the same: learn the fundamentals well, know your opponent or their style, prepare for the unexpected, and take the initiative. That is how you learn to become truly great in kendo.

Funada (Hong Kong A) attempts a men

THE 14TH HONG KONG ASIAN OPEN KENDO CHAMPIONSHIPS March 1-2, 2014

By Dr. Stephen Robert Nagy
Photos by Bonnie Ngan

I. Introduction

When we think of prestigious kendo tournaments, the World Kendo Championships (WKC), the All Japan Kendo Championships, and other major competitions held in Japan usually spring to mind. These are events in which we can see the best kendo in the world, but there are other important locations where kendo is being practised and demonstrated at very high levels. More importantly, the level that is being exhibited at these tournaments outside of Japan is improving thanks to the leadership of various kendo organisations, and the many teachers in the world that not only dedicate themselves to passing on

Left to right: Ujiie-sensei, Yano-sensei, Lai-sensei, Sumi-sensei

the traditions of kendo, but are committed to fostering excellence in their students.

This article will introduce some of the highlights of the 14th Hong Kong Asian Open Kendo Championships (HKAOKC). Organized by the Hong Kong Kendo Association (HKKA) and supported by the International Kendo Federation (FIK), the tournament's initial purpose was to expose participants to competitive kendo. Since the first tournament 14 years ago, it has become an important kendo training ground in East Asia that has grown from a small regional tournament attracting mostly teams in the immediate region, to a competition that draws teams from all over Southeast Asia, Australia, Japan and Korea.

II. The event

Every year, the FIK dispatches kendo teachers from Japan to act as judges and representatives. This ensures that participants have a chance to meet, talk, and train with Japan's top sensei. At the same time, these visits provide the sensei and the FIK with a sense of the development and internationalisation of kendo in different parts of the world.

This year, the HKKA was fortunate to have had two official teachers dispatched to the tournament: H8-dan Yano Hiroshi-sensei, the famed Kokushikan University teacher, and K8-dan Ujiie Michio-sensei, also of Kokushikan University, who has since been awarded Hanshi. Also in attendance were Fukuoka University of Education's H8-dan Sumi Masatake-sensei, a regular supporter of the HKAOKC, and Hong Kong's only K8-dan teacher, Roberto Kishikawa-sensei. Participants in the tournament had the opportunity to engage in *keiko* with these accomplished sensei twice a day during the two-day tournament, at 7am and then again in the afternoon following the competition.

This year's tournament featured teams from China, Macau, Chinese Taipei, Russia, Australia, Japan, Korea, Kazakhstan, India, Singapore, Malaysia, Indonesia, Thailand, Vietnam, Philippines and Hong Kong. It consisted of three divisions: a ladies' open three-person team tournament (33 participants); a men's 3-dan and under three-person team tournament (48 participants); and a men's open five-person team tournament (65 participants).

III. Dan Examination

The two-day competition was preceded by a grading, and as in previous years, eligible kendoka were able to grade from shodan through to 5-dan. In line with examinations around the world, the number of successful candidates dropped sharply in the 4-dan and 5-dan gradings (see results below). The judges commented that the general competency of examinees for the lower grades has increased, but that there is still much work to do in terms of mastering essential skills such as *seme* in order to achieve success in 4-dan and 5-dan.

The third-placed Hong Kong team with Kishikawa-sensei

Dan Exam Results:					
	shodan	2-dan	3-dan	4-dan	5-dan
Total:	58	33	28	14	6
Pass:	54	28	14	5	3
Fail:	2	4	14	9	3
Absent:	2	1	0	0	0

IV. The Ladies' Open Three-Person Team Event

The women's event on Saturday featured competitors from around the region, and many had participated in the last WKC. Experience at the highest level of kendo competition resulted in some exciting and competitive matches. This year's final featured IGA Kendo Club A (Philippines) and All Japan Budogu (Japan). The IGA team battled valiantly, but ultimately the All Japan Budogu team was victorious. The fact that a team from the Philippines made it to the final reflects the increased popularity and improvement of kendo throughout Southeast Asian countries.

The third-place finishers in this year's tournament hailed from Hong Kong and New South Wales, Australia. Due to the solid performances from all of the women's teams, the judges deemed that eight players from eight different teams be given the Fighting Spirit Award.

V. The Men's 3-dan and Under Three-Person Team Event

Like the ladies' tournament, the men's 3-dan and under three-person team tournament also featured former participants of the WKC, such as Hong Kong's MJ Lee and Australia's Jayson Chaplin. The New South Wales A team came first in a highly competitive match with the Vietnam A team. Korea's KKF team tied with the Guangzhou Zhixin Kendo Club A team for third place.

VI. The Men's Open Five-Person Team Event

This year was my second time competing in the 5-man team competition and I could immediately sense the improvement in the strength of teams and their diversity, as the strong teams were no longer only from Japan. The results speak for themselves, with the Korean Kumdo Association's (KKA) AKKC team soundly defeating most of the opponents they faced until the semi-finals. Their aggressive style and skilful techniques led them to their first title by defeating the Shanghai Kendo Club A team in a thrilling final that was decided by a *daihyō-sen*. Their path to victory did not come easily though, as in the semi-finals they met the Thailand A team led by 7-dan Morisaki Seichiro. Fighting toe-to-toe, Morisaki stunned his opponent and the audience with an amazing *gyaku-kaeshi-dō* making their trip to the finals a hard fought match.

As in previous years, the Hong Kong A team represented the host city with a very strong performance. As a mixed team that consisted of two Japanese who were

New South Wales' Jayson Chaplin

Joshua Chan (Hong Kong A) stands toe-to-toe with his opponent

living and working in Hong Kong as well as three locals, they finished in third-place, demonstrating great heart, determination and teamwork.

VII. Behind the Scenes: Sensei, Referees and Helpers

In every tournament that I have attended, the competition seems to flow effortlessly. What was noticeable about the 14th HKAOKC was the inclusion of many helpers of various rank and the enlistment of high ranking sensei from Hong Kong and participating countries. It was clear that the HKKA and competition organisers made stakeholders of the entire Hong Kong kendo community by enlisting junior kendoka, young teenagers, and those new to kendo. Some helped set up the courts for fighting, others worked as timers and others helped clean up after the fighters had gone home. They were exposed to the scoring system, how to set up courts, manage players and various other essential tasks that make a successful kendo competition.

Horibe-sensei (7-dan) working alongside the next generation of referees

Tournament referees

David Graham assisting with the scoreboard

This inclusion in kendo activities in Hong Kong is representative of a broader view amongst the HKKA and teachers in Hong Kong that kendo is not just about the competition or training every week, it is actually much more holistic. In order to cultivate good kendoka in the region, there is a need to expose them, no matter what their age or level is, to all aspects of kendo. It is through this exposure that kendoka can learn various facets that make kendo so rich.

A case in point was young David Graham, a Scottish national living and practising kendo in Hong Kong. Although only 12 years old, David was given the opportunity to cultivate a different side of his kendo by helping set up the scoreboards with his senpai. It may seem insignificant, but these kind of initiatives help to internationalise kendo by cultivating its human resources that can then help pass on the plethora of traditions that are part-and-parcel of kendo.

Aside from the important and numerous volunteers that make the competition happen, we must also recognise the contributions of the sensei who act as coaches and sometimes as counsellors when results do not meet expectations.

Like most players, we do not want to win or lose because of a bad call by a referee. The HKAOKC is especially fortunate in this regard, as many high ranking sensei from the region actively contribute to the tournament's success by participating as referees, by passing on their experience as referees, and ensuring that the players receive the best judging possible.

The HKAOKC demonstrated this philosophy throughout the tournament with the final of the Men's Open Five-Person Team-event that was adjudicated by Ujiie-sensei. He provided the highest level of refereeing to ensure that the competitors could compete against each other with complete confidence.

VIII. Conclusion

With the 16th WKC a little under a year away in May 2015, we should expect that the 15th and 16th HKAOKC will be the final proving grounds for those kendoka and teams wishing to compete with the best teams in the region prior to them facing teams on a global scale. Reflecting on the development and growth of kendo as seen in the HKAOKC over the past few years, we should definitely expect outstanding performances from kendoka in the region and the continued internationalisation of kendo.

*Thank you to the Hong Kong Kendo Association for their help and materials related to the tournament.

The Greater Meaning of Kendo

Reidan-jichi Part 17
Kihon-dōsa: No. 6

By Prof. Ōya Minoru (Kendo Kyōshi 7-dan)
International Budo University

Translated by Alex Bennett
Some sections of the text incorporate previous translations of Ōya-sensei's work by Steven Harwood

Kirikaeshi

1. The Meaning and Benefits of *Kirikaeshi*

Kirikaeshi is an indispensable exercise in kendo that combines *shōmen* strikes with left and right *men* strikes. It is a basic exercise that contains all of the important technical elements of kendo, and is a useful means for fixing bad habits that may have crept into your basic skills set. It is absolutely vital to include *kirikaeshi* into your training regime, regardless of what rank you hold. It is one of the most important basic training methods in kendo. The main objectives of *kirikaeshi* are as follows:

To develop :
1. Correct posture and *kamae*
2. Understanding of *maai* (the spatial interval between you and your opponent)
3. Footwork and body movement
4. Use of the upper limbs for swinging the *shinai* correctly
5. Synchronization of the feet and *shinai* when striking
6. Correct trajectory and line of attack (*hasuji*)
7. *Tenouchi* (grip) and muscle manipulation in the hands
8. Flexibility in the wrists for directing the *shinai*
9. Breathing technique
10. *Zanshin* (lingering mind)

2. How to do Kirikaeshi

1. Assume *chūdan*,
2. Strike *shōmen* (centre *men*) from *issoku-ittō-no-maai* (one-step, one-sword interval)
3. After *shōmen*, strike *hidari-men* (partner's left *men*) followed by *migi-men* consecutively (four strikes forward, five strikes while going back)
4. Assume *chūdan* again
5. Strike *shōmen* from *issoku-ittō-no-maai* (this is the entire sequence, and it is usually repeated twice)
6. After *shōmen*, strike *hidari-men* (partner's left *men*) followed by *migi-men* consecutively (four strikes forward, five strikes while going back)
7. Assume *chūdan* again
8. Strike *shōmen* from *issoku-ittō-no-maai*
9. After running through, demonstrate *zanshin*

{Points to take note of}
1. Your *kamae* must be correct from the outset, and do not compromise your posture throughout the entire sequence.
2. Start by doing each strike in a "large" and "precise" motion, and as you get better at it, make the strikes "large", "strong", "fast", and "nimble".

3. The muscles in your upper body should be limber, not tense. In order to make the swings adequate, and ensure that the line of each cut (*hasuji*) is correct, be sure to lift your left hand directly overhead for each swing.
4. When striking left and right *men*, the hands are crossed with each cut with the angle of the *shinai* at 45°, cutting with the "blade" edge, not the sides.
5. Be sure to strike the target (*men*) accurately with the *monouchi* of the *shinai*. You should not end up with empty strikes, or aim for the partner's *shinai*. Aim for *men*.
6. Even though the left hand is raised up and down vertically in the swings, it should never veer away from the centreline of the body. At the point of contact for each strike, the left hand is positioned at the height of the solar-plexus.
7. Moving forward and back while striking should be done with *okuri-ashi*. It is particularly important to take care after finishing the four steps forward and starting to go back, as footwork often becomes confused at this point. It is useful to take the first step back from the left foot as big as possible.
8. Furthermore, to avoid *ayumi-ashi* when going back, try to make each step back with the left foot as big as you can.
9. Do not bounce up and down by straightening your legs as you make each strike, and refrain from creating a rhythm to your strikes with your lower back and head. In other words, keep on an even keel as you go forward and back.
10. Make sure that you continue with the same breath after making the first *shōmen* strike.

3. Receiving Kirikaeshi

The receiver is not just a striking-dummy for the attacker. The receiver has a responsibility to facilitate the attacker's improvement, and to control the exercise so that it can be done properly. In this sense, the receiver should be aware that they occupy the role of "instructor". There are two main ways for receiving strikes: "pulling in" (*hikikomu*), and "striking down" (*uchiotosu*). With this in mind, the following points should be adhered to when receiving *kirikaeshi*:

1. Hikikomu

The "pulling in" method for receiving is used for encouraging the attacker to stretch out as they strike, and is particularly useful when teaching beginners to make big, accurate striking movements. The *shinai* should be held vertically with both hands, and the hands transferred alternately to the left and right side of the body while receiving each strike to that side. At the same time, pull the attacker's *shinai* in as it connects with yours, encouraging them to extend their arms further as they strike. That way, their strikes will be able to reach further, and they will learn correct *tenouchi* at the point of contact.

2. Uchiotosu

By striking the *shinai* down as it makes contact, the attacker learns when to relax, and when to tense their hands in the strike, and also how to use the upper body efficiently. This method is mainly used when receiving *kirikaeshi* for more advanced practitioners. The *shinai* is transferred alternately from left to right at the diagonal front, and goes to meet the incoming strike, hitting the attacker's *shinai* down (not excessively) on impact. This way, the attacker learns correct *tenouchi* in the strike, and also how to maintain flexibility in the upper body and arms to keep the momentum going from side to side. Take care, however, not to strike down too hard, or too early, as this will ruin the attacker's form, and will make it a futile exercise.

When receiving using both *hikikomu* and *uchiotosu*, it is important to focus on *tenouchi* with each moment of contact.

{Points to take note of}

1. Get your feeling in sync with the attacker, and make it easy for them to strike.
2. With the first strike to *shōmen*, receive the blow with the *kensen* slightly to the side from the interval of *issoku-ittō-no-maai*.
3. Receive when moving backwards and forwards using *ayumi-ashi*. The foot on the side you are receiving should be at the rear. Always be aware of the distance so that the attacker is able to extend out but still strike with the correct part of the *shinai*. Also, receive in harmony with the vigour of the attacker's strike and the timing.
4. The *shinai* is held vertically, and the strikes are received on the *shinogi* (side) of the *monouchi*. The left hand is positioned around hip height making sure that the hands are not lifted too high.
5. Taking into consideration the level of the attacker, receive by pulling the attacker forward when you are moving back, and with the feeling of pushing them back when you are moving forward. This will encourage the attacker to work hard with their footwork and striking as they adapt to the change.
6. When receiving the very last *shōmen* strike, do not move out of the way immediately. Instead, move back two or three steps as the strike is made to urge the attacker to keep moving forward, and then move to the right to let them run through.

"Shobu wa saya no uchi"

(Victory attained with the sword still sheathed.)

Hayashizaki Jinsuke Shigenobu (1559?-1604?) lived around the beginning of the Tokugawa period (1603-1868) and is widely known as the creator of the sword drawing art of iaido. He established the Shin-Musō Hayashizaki-ryū.

"The purpose of iai is to not cut, nor be cut by the enemy. It is a way of peace which requires considerable discipline."

Iai (*iaijutsu*) originally described an actual form of combat. The appellation was used in reference to the technique of drawing one's sword in a flash to cut down an enemy about to attack. In accordance with the teaching, "*Tsune ni ite, kyū ni awasu*", which translates along the lines of "being constantly 'prepared' (i) to 'meet' (ai) the enemy in an instant", the *iai* encounter was all over in the blink of an eye. The sword was removed from its scabbard so quickly and effectively that the woeful recipient of the blow could not possibly know what had struck him. *Iai* was also called *battō-jutsu*, which simply means "draw the blade". The point was to end the encounter before the opponent had a chance to unsheathe his own sword. If the enemy was afforded enough time to brandish his sword, too, the engagement then becomes *kenjutsu*, or sword against sword. Technically speaking, that is why *iai*, by definition, demanded that "Victory is attained with the [enemy's] sword still sheathed." But, this also had a more profound, peaceful, philosophical implication.

The series of popular film, manga and TV stories called "*The Lone Wolf and Cub*" feature a formidable samurai called Ogami Ittō, and his infant son. Ogami was a master of the Suiō-ryū school of swordsmanship, a style that was created by Mima Yoichizaemon. When Yoichizaemon was 18, his father's friend, Sakurai Goroemon Naomitsu, came to visit. Knowing of Naomitsu's sublime skills in swordsmanship, Yoichizaemon asked for a "friendly" duel. Naomitsu was happy to oblige. When the duel started, Naomitsu kept his sword sheathed, and as Yoichizaemon approached and assumed the overhead posture (*jōdan*), Naomitsu's blade was suddenly in his face. It was an exhibition of *iaijutsu*.

The sword was drawn in a nanosecond, and Naomitsu's show of skill would change Yoichizaemon's life. Naomitsu was in fact a disciple of Hayashizaki Jinsuke Shigenobu, the man largely accepted as the founder of iaido. Yoichizaemon humbly became a student of Naomitsu and soaked up his teachings like a sponge.

One day when Yoichizaemon was travelling the countryside seeking would-be opponents to hone his skills, he arrived at Tsuyama in Misa-no-Kuni. He started gathering students to teach the art of *iai*. Another swordsman called Asada Kurobei was also active in the region, and not being overly enthused about a new kid on the block poaching students, a match was imminent. One of Asada's followers asked his master, "How can you possibly defeat Mima Yoichizamon's *iai*?" Asada replied, "I will make him draw his sword out, then defeat him." Hearing of Asada's strategy, Yoichizaemon realised it was a match he had no chance of winning. Evidently, Asada knew how to take the sting away from *iai* by nullifying the draw. This story is slightly misleading, as any *iai* exponent was also a *kenjutsu* expert as well. Plan B was always a prerequisite. Hayashizaki Jinsuke Shigenobu's eminence throughout the land is testimony to this.

The life and career of Hayashizaki Jinsuke Shigenobu is somewhat vague, and it is hard to know which of the abounding legends is true. One well known story concerns his mission to exact revenge for the death of his father. To this end, he made a pilgrimage to either the Shinmei or Hiyoshi Shrine and engaged in a rigorous regime of ascetic training – praying, meditating, and swinging a sword around. Eventually, his efforts paid off, and he was visited by a deity in a dream and taught the "secret techniques" of *iaijutsu*, which he called *battō-jutsu*. It worked. His father was avenged in a flash and a whistle of his blade. Results speak for themselves, and he amassed many disciples. His school was known by various different names such as Junpaku-den, Hayashizaki-ryū, Shin Musō Hayashizaki-Ryū, and so on.

This was about the time when warriors stopped wearing their swords dangling from the side with the blade facing down, and started inserting them firmly in their belts with the blade up. This meant it could be drawn in a very swift movement called *nuki-tsuke*, utilising the right hand to flick the sword out as the left hand simultaneously pulled the scabbard back. It was akin to the technique used by gunslingers in the Old West, who were mind-bogglingly fast on the draw. Think Wild Bill Hickok. Well, that was actually Hayashizaki Jinsuke Shigenobu with a hat and a pistol.

By
ALEX BENNETT
Based on the book
"KENSHI NO MEIGON" (1998)
by the late Tobe Shinjūrō
Used with author's permission.

Jinsuke is recorded as having made two *musha-shugyō* pilgrimages in his lifetime, and gathered a number of talented students, many of whom went on to make their own illustrious schools of *iaijutsu*. Tamiya Taira-no-Hyōe Narimasa was also one of his students who founded the Tamiya-ryū, and is thought to have taught three generations of shoguns, Tokugawa Ieyasu, Hidetada and Iemitsu.

One of the most popular styles of iaido in the modern day is the Musō Jikiden Eishin-ryū. This school was created by Hasegawa Chikaranosuke Hidenobu (Eishin), seven generations after Jinsuke, and is known as a school of subtle techniques and panache, but still retaining the original, highly practical nature of the source of the stream. His legacy is seen in most schools of iaido in existence today. Shin Musō Hayashizaki-ryū, however, is no longer with us…

Nevertheless, the real secret of Jinsuke's *iai* was to defeat the opponent without having to draw the sword. This was achieved by being a totally nice guy, but still having the ability to rip strips off a stroppy contender. He emphasised the importance of living life without causing ire, and treating others respectfully, and with sincerity. His mantra was, "The purpose of *iai* is to not cut, nor be cut by the enemy. It is a way of peace which requires considerable discipline."

Indeed, as was the trend with hardened warriors who excelled among their peers in the turbulent times of feudal Japan, "peace" became a sacred word. Many of the hard-core killers eventually had epiphanies about the importance of life over death. Still, the talk had to be backed up with the walk. Avoiding conflict was a choice, and by no means a case of chickenitis. But, winning without actual conflict became the ultimate objective of *iaijustu*, and remains so in iaido today.

KENDO IN THE SNOW

Text and photos by Magnus Johansson, Shimbukan Skellefteå Budo Club

From February 21-23, 2014, the 1st Annual Swedish Kangeiko was held in Skellefteå, Sweden. Kendoka from Sweden, Norway, England, Wales, and Hungary gathered for a weekend of kendo training at Skellefteå Budokan. Shimbukan Skellefteå Budo Club organised the seminar that was led by Hungarian sensei Tibor Bárány, 7-dan. During the weekend, six training sessions were held focusing on everything from basic footwork to *shiai* and *kata*, which provided the participants with a good mix of serious and fun exercises.

Obviously, being *kan-geiko*, a short session was also held outside–around 20 minutes of *keiko* in the snow done with bare feet! It included *kirikaeshi*, *waza* practice, *ji-geiko* and *ippon-shōbu*, and was documented by several photographers, which provided material for some crazy Facebook updates for all the participants. After the outdoor *kan-geiko* session, a traditional (mixed) Swedish sauna warmed frozen limbs and prepared everyone for more indoor training.

For the Sayonara Party, a rather wet winter barbecue was held on the snow-clad roof of a four-storey building. It was probably a bit dangerous, but great fun nonetheless.

The 1st Annual Swedish Kangeiko was organised by Shimbukan Skellefteå Budo Club. This club has about 50 members and a kendo history going back more than 20 years. Despite its remote location, the club has been ranked as one of the top three clubs in Sweden for more than ten years. The club is based at Skellefteå Budokan, a newly built centre that holds three dojo shared by seven clubs that practise aikido, iaido, jodo, judo, jujutsu, kendo, kyudo and karate. Currently, three members are in the Swedish national team and two attend the International Budo University in Katsuura, Japan.

Skellefteå, a small town with a population of 70,000,

Shimbukan winter swimming

is in the remote part of northern Sweden. It has a strong history of winter sports including the Snowmobile World Championships, European Ski Cup and the (slightly mental) Swedish Open Winter Swimming Championships. This is held in the frozen river next to Skellefteå Budokan, and Shimbukan's own swimming team has previously finished in the top 10.

Kan-geiko in 2015 is now being planned, again with a high-ranked guest sensei, and we would love to have participants from all over the world. Held in January, you can expect lots of snow and rather cold weather (around -25°C/-13°F). Travel here by car, bus, train or aeroplane to either Skellefteå or Umeå airports. Arrive a few days early or stay a bit longer and Shimbukan will arrange a place to sleep and take you out for a spin in the snow. This might include downhill skiing, outdoor cooking, winter fishing and/or a snowmobile safari where you could encounter elk and reindeer. With a little luck, at night you might also get to see the aurora borealis, or Northern Lights. With all this on offer, what's to stop you from joining us?

Follow us on Facebook (Kangeiko - Shimbukan) for more info about the upcoming camp and how to sign up. We hope to see you in 2015!

The British participants getting to grips with the snow

An Innovative Method for Kendo Shiai:
Bringing out the Best

By Motohiro KIHARA (Naruto University of Education), Masurao KUSAMA (Hiroshima University), Naoya YOKOYAMA (Yokohama National University), Takao BANDO (Osaka University)

It goes without saying that kendo players do not want to get hit during a match. To this end, many adopt defensive postures to negate the opponent's attack. Although such poses do not infringe the rules of competition, they detract from the quality and spirit of kendo. Our research group conducted an experiment in which college-level kendo competitors engaged in matches, but were also judged according to the postures they assumed during the bouts. Their comments and opinions were collated to assess the viability of a new adjudication system for kendo matches. This research was presented at the 45th Japanese Academy of Budo Convention in 2013, and published in the ensuing proceedings. This report is based on our original paper, and we hope that people in the international kendo community will consider our ideas, which were designed to uphold the integrity of kendo as a sport and a way for developing character.

The tentative plan we came up with is as follows: A "judging referee" (*hantei-shinpan-in*) also observed and adjudicated the match in addition to the usual formation of chief referee and assistant referees. If the match was not decided by a valid strike (*yūkō-datotsu*) or through *hansoku* in the stipulated time, the outcome hinged on the decision of the "judging referee". The judging referee did not base his/her verdict on the "superiority of player's technique and posture", but rather on the least number of "inferior posture points" (*shisei-ketten*).

As the "judging referee" was seated and observing the matches from outside the court, "inferior posture points" could be assessed without the need to interrupt the flow of the match. A scoreboard similar to those used in table tennis matches was used to show the points to all people involved in the match, including the players, referees, and spectators. If the number of "inferior posture points" was also equal at the end of regulation time, the match was extended for two-minutes (*enchō*).

The pictures in Figure 1 show examples of "inferior posture points" that were identified during matches.

❶ Defence posture with three points covered
❷ Close positioning for self-defence
❸ Defence with broken posture after hitting
❹ Unsightly defence posture after hitting
❺ Squatting just before the match area boundary line
❻ A fall

Figure 1. Examples of "inferior posture points" (shisei-ketten)

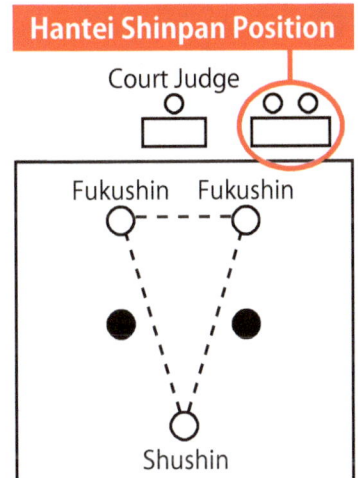

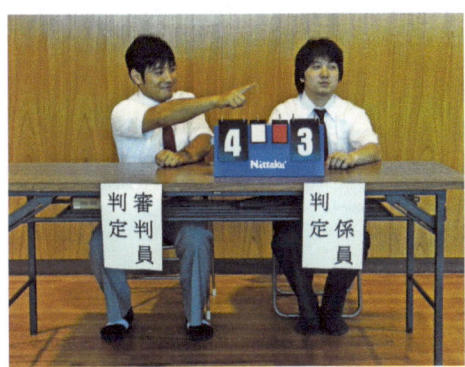

Figure 2. Position of the "Hantei Shinpan" (left)

Overall, the competitors were generally positive about the trial. Some comments included: "It encourages us to try not to break our posture during the match", "Matches progressed smoothly", "Matches hardly went into extra time", and "The new system is effective for encouraging reflection about the content of the match". Some of the negative comments included: "The criteria of the new system were not clear", "It is difficult to judge the reflexive defence as an inferior point", "The posture with both arms raised above the head (jōdan-no-kamae) is advantageous", and "The scoreboard is distracting". The results of our experiment indicated that with a few improvements, such an innovative system could be used to improve the quality of kendo matches, and also encourage competitors to reflect on their habits, form, and attitude in *shiai*.

References
- Ōtsuka, T., "Sengo kendō no rūru keisei katei no kenkyū", *Research Journal of Budo*, 22(2), 51-52, 1986.
- Ōtsuka, T., *Kenshi ni tsugu - Nihon kendo no mirai no tame ni –*, Mado-sha, 2005.
- Takizawa, K., "Kendō shiai oyobi shinpan-kitei ni kansuru kenkyū", *Research Journal of Budo*, 4(1), 15, 1971

WHAT'S THIS ABOUT THE NEW RULES FOR BLOCKING?

By Andy Fisher

A few months ago there was a lot of discussion among the internet kendo community about the introduction of some new rules for junior high school level *shiai* in Japan, and the topic recently resurfaced on the Kendo World forums. Basically, the rule addresses young practitioners who use an overly defensive strategy in matches in order to avoid losing points, particularly by employing a defensive stance.

As someone who is regularly practising with some of Japan's top-level, competitive junior high and high school kendoka, as well as their respective teachers, this is something that will directly affect the kendo community that I am involved in. I therefore took great interest in the introduction of the new rules, and read all the information currently available in both English and Japanese. Moreover, what has been interesting is the generally positive reaction from the international kendo community, with many practitioners hoping that the same rules will also be applied to adult tournaments.

At this point, I think it is also important to mention that another rule change was implemented in high school level matches in 2009. This rule was in regard to *tsubazeriai*, and was put in place to stop competitive players using it to kill time, or to execute deceitful techniques. This rule change was a success, and the quality of kendo in both the high school and university levels is already improving. I believe that it could easily be implemented in all levels of *shiai* without any negative effects.

As noted above, many of the English-language responses that I have read regarding the new junior high school rule change have been in favour of it. However, I cannot help but feel that this is possibly because it is being slightly misinterpreted by most. Many seem to think that this rule will stop players from raising their arms to defend *men*, *kote* and *dō* when they are put under pressure. On closer inspection, the reality is actually somewhat different.

To be clear, here is my translation of what the official document states:

> When an "unusual" stance is assumed, after *gōgi*, a warning will be given in the first instance. On the second occurrence, again after *gōgi*, a *hansoku* (penalty) shall be awarded.

This is indeed vague, so the document continues:

> In reference to the shared understanding of "unusual" stances:
> 1– An "unusual" stance is when the left fist is raised to a height which is approximately above the eye line, in order to protect the *men*, *right-kote* and *right-dō*, all at the same time.

 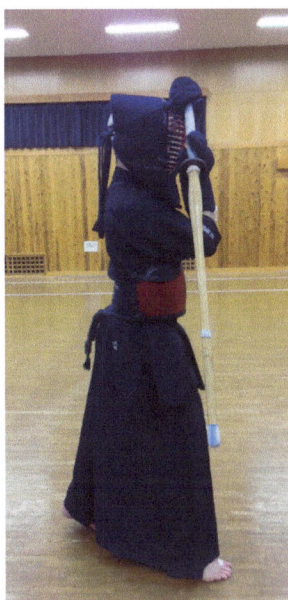

This seems to be quite straightforward, but I believe it is still open to misinterpretation. The key, I think, is that in the Japanese text the term *kamae* (構え) is mainly used to describe this action. For this reason, I believe that the rule is referring to people taking this stance as a method of continual defence. In other words, spending more time in that position than in other fighting postures, and does not refer to the act of spontaneous blocking.

The article continues:

> 2– In the following cases, a warning or hansoku is NOT given:
> - When the posture is taken from *chūdan-no-kamae* in order to execute *ōji-waza*.
> - When the posture is assumed after receiving physical pressure in *tsubazeriai* or from *taiatari*, or when the posture has been assumed momentarily as the result of the opponent's *seme*.

These points illustrate the times when a warning or *hansoku* is NOT given, and it is particularly the latter that grabs my attention. Basically, it says you can assume the defensive posture (referred to as *sanshō-yoke*) if you do so as a result of your opponent's physical pressure, or more importantly, *seme*. This means, by these rules it is permissible to momentarily assume *sanshō-yoke* to block strikes if you fear you will be struck. It is here where I believe that many people are perhaps mistaken in the interpretation of this rule, as many people seem to think that it somehow outlaws blocking, which it simply does not.

The purpose of this rule's introduction starts to become a little more apparent in the following section:

> 3– Points for consideration:
> - Because there are many cases when the left fist is close to being above eye level, but not actually above it, it is essential that the position of the left fist is checked each time the position is assumed.
> - When a player takes an unusual stance and waits for their opponent to strike, if a strike is then made from that position, it will not be considered as *ōji-waza*.

It can be assumed that the real reason for implementing this is to stop players from constantly using the *sanshō-yoke* posture as an alternative to *chūdan-no-kamae*; not to stop them from raising their arm to block when put under pressure. When you take into consideration that *chūdan-no-kamae* is the only fighting posture allowed at junior high school level, and that *tsuki* techniques are not allowed either, it is easy to imagine how some youngsters were using this posture to avoid defeat.

For the above reasons, I personally feel that these rules do not need to be implemented in adult *shiai*, as adults have more options of dealing with an opponent in the *sanshō-yoke* posture than junior high school children do. When we also consider what is covered by these rules, very few adults continually stand in this posture in order to avoid being hit during *shiai*. Certainly, adults who are good at winning *shiai* do not seem to adopt this strategy.

To conclude, if the question is, "Should we implement these rules as they are into adult kendo?" my personal response would be that of indifference, as I honestly do not think that it will change much. However, if the question becomes, "Should we ban blocking?" well, that is a whole different discussion…

Kendo That Cultivates People

by Sumi Masatake (Hanshi 8-dan)
Translated by Honda Sōtarō

Part 16
Teaching Kendo to the Next Generation

In the previous instalment I described ideal kendo training with an emphasis on the psychological aspects of technique acquisition. I stressed the cultivation of strong willpower so that practitioners do not fear the *kensen* of *motodachi* or shy away from hard practice. I also mentioned that respect and courtesy are necessary so that traits such as gratitude, modesty and sincerity can be developed in one's interpersonal relationships. In this instalment I will focus on how interpersonal relationships cultivate the mind of the individual. The development of our mind is closely connected to the level of our growth and maturity, and ideally the mind should be nourished with content that varies according to the different stages of its development. Instructors must be very careful not to obstruct or delay the mental development of their students.

The beginning of mental cultivation and the forging of interpersonal relationships

The proverb "as the boy, so the man" reminds us of the importance of discipline for young children. However, in recent times I feel that many parents are overprotective of their children and may be doing more harm than good. Children have always been considered a blessing upon their parents, but this did not lead those of past times to dote upon their children and excessively spoil them. Those of yesteryear raised their children with strict discipline and concern for their future. Eastern and Western cultures both agree that a child's innate potential for self-development and growth is best stimulated with an even balance of parental affection and discipline during infancy. Children therefore should be disciplined properly from an early stage and positive behaviour should be praised. If a child who behaves well is praised, they will learn what appropriate behaviour is and repeat that behaviour to receive praise again. This is the start of character building, and it is essential that parents demonstrate courtesy and manners at home and set an example for children to follow. When children are going through rebellious stages, parents need to insist more firmly upon good manners and personal responsibility. Unacceptable behaviour should not be tolerated but, on the other hand, parents should avoid assisting their child too much in life, as this may stifle the development of their child's independence.

Kendo can provide discipline to young children so the aim of training should not just be to practise techniques, nor should techniques just be acquired as a basis for competing against others. To produce outstanding youth through kendo, we must teach them as children to be well-mannered and have open and accepting hearts. For a sapling to develop and grow strong roots, the soil must be in good condition; likewise it is difficult to cultivate children if there are negative influences or temptations in their life. Consequently I do not believe that kendo competitions should be held for young children due to the negative pressure that winning and losing has on young minds.

If we praise young children when they display good manners, carry themselves with good posture, and pay attention to their seniors, they will become motivated and will look forward to coming back to the dojo, and through this process of development they will acquire self-discipline. I hope that kendo teachers praise and cultivate their students and that parents support teachers in this endeavour.

Interpersonal relationships that foster confidence in children

Children are malleable only for so long, so it is best to begin nurturing and training them as early as possible, well before they begin reaching adolescence. The adolescent mind begins to scheme and make compromises, while the purer mind of the younger child is more sincere and less calculating. Pre-adolescents may often want to spend more time with their peers than with their parents, and this can be of understandable concern. At this time they need to be shown the correct path to follow in preparation for their adult life and must be encouraged to be independent. Ideally a child should experience open and accepting relationships that foster self-consciousness and self-awareness, and in doing so they will be able to better judge their own actions and behaviour, and in turn feel valued and appreciated. Parents should take care that children are not influenced negatively by the bad behaviour and attitudes of adults, which may cause them apprehension or loss of confidence.

People who start kendo as children need to be made aware that at the *nyūmon-ki* stage one must simply learn the basics correctly. Teachers therefore should give little regard to competition and recognise and praise the efforts of children trying to learn the basics correctly. Naturally, training in this period is not always enjoyable and young students may not be aware of the progress they are making, so teachers need to encourage young students to feel a sense of fulfilment in being totally absorbed in attacking the *motodachi*, and a sense of

achievement through participating in hard *kirikaeshi* and *uchikomi* training. The confidence and self-esteem of students will be bolstered if their teacher appreciates their efforts.

When students successfully pass *kyū* or *dan* examinations, teachers should have students reflect upon the training processes that allowed them to succeed rather than just being pleased with their results. In kendo we achieve progress with the help of our teacher, our *motodachi*, and our training partners; not just our own efforts. Hence we should thank these people as well as congratulate ourselves. Once students recognise and accept that mutual respect and support are the key to progress in kendo, then, with the encouragement of their teacher, they can finally find themselves commencing "real" kendo training. Naturally this is just the beginning, and many lessons remain for the young practitioner in their quest for personal cultivation. If achieving a *dan* grade in junior high school or winning a *shiai* at high school is the highlight of a kendo practitioner's training, then these fleeting achievements will soon fade from memory as will the hard efforts they made to achieve

Interpersonal relationships that cultivate independent learning

The advice "let your children see the world" acknowledges that we must encourage children to leave the safe confines of the family nest and seek out challenging new environments so that they may become independent. From late teens to early twenties, youths need to forge the skills they will use later in adult relationships. They will face a variety of new experiences and will be involved in conflicts involving people in various levels of hierarchy, and as such will be exposed to both unfairness and hypocrisy. By late adolescence, when many teenagers are entering the workforce, they need to experience larger-scale emotional dynamics than those experienced in early adolescence. I often feel that this is what is lacking in the youth of today. I find myself viewing certain young adults as flowers who were carefully tended to in protective greenhouses and are not prepared for the harsh environment of reality outside.

Naturally, as parents and teachers we wish to provide familiarity and comfort for children but being overprotective is doing them a disservice. We often misjudge what is required to build self-esteem and dignity in children. The youth of today are often distressed as they live in a society that is rapidly changing and have to deal with so much information. We need educational environments that place emphasis on the integrity and inner harmony of the individual in an uncompromising manner. Attempting to teach in a scientifically efficient manner or, taking the opposite extreme, leaving students to their own devices, stunts their true growth as individuals and inhibits their sense of self-identity. I believe that the overload principle used in muscular development can be applied to the development of the mind as well. In kendo we often hear the saying *hyaku-ren-ji-toku* (repeated practice is required to master a technique) and we must experience both physical and mental overload to fully develop as individuals.

Teacher-student relations still exist in traditional arts and crafts today. In trying to emulate the skills of their teacher, the student should not stand around idly waiting for instruction as, in some extreme cases, the teacher will not volunteer any instruction at all. Students must try to learn for themselves whilst mimicking their teacher, as their teacher is a student in their own right who is still trying to develop their own skills to a higher level. In certain cases, the teacher will not offer explanation or advice but simply criticise the poor work of the student. In such strict relationships, only the students who have been consistently patient will inherit the school from their teacher and be allowed to carry on the tradition,

those goals. *Shinsa* and *shiai* are just two small facets of the greater kendo whole that only amount to scratching the surface in terms of mental cultivation.

The teacher-student relationship is a crucial facet in mental development. If a teacher and student have a quality relationship based on mutual respect, then it is possible for a teacher to reprimand a student for their performance despite having won a *shiai*, and it is also possible to praise their performance despite them having lost. If a teacher builds an interactive relationship with their students to allow a healthy exchange of questions and answers, then those students will grow as individuals whereas they would be stunted if they were only given instructions and reprimands.

thus ensuring the quality of the school's successors.

Even while under the guidance of a teacher, it is still important to cultivate oneself in an independent manner. If an individual aims to cultivate their mental strength through the acquisition of techniques, they then need to leave the safe confines of their place of learning and put themselves in high-pressure environments where tough demands will be made of them. As they progress into larger clubs, such as those at university level, they will be required to tackle training involving a high level of formality and a rigid hierarchy system where there is a respectful relationship distance kept from *shihan*, club teachers, coaches, and senior students. The basic foundations for cultivation of the mind can be found in the junior student experience, and later, as a senior student, the mind is cultivated through learning opportunities from the *shihan*, club teachers, and coaches.

Junior students are expected to be obedient towards senior students, but mindlessly obeying every order in a "yes-man" fashion will not allow them to grow. However, not cooperating outright with an instruction equates with denying your training. Although the junior student is in a difficult position, they must be aware of their own thoughts and feelings whilst following orders because unquestionably following their seniors is of no benefit to their growth and they might as well give up. Obedience to your teachers and seniors is part of training and you will develop and improve if you diligently follow their advice and train hard. This process builds a firm foundation in practitioners and, if techniques are acquired through wholehearted effort while stressed and under pressure, you will come to develop a stable mind.

Naturally the attitudes of the *shihan*, club teachers, coaches, and senior students, and the manner in which they oversee club members, is of vital importance. Those in positions of authority must be fair and observe each individual club member to train them in a individually appropriate manner. If those in teaching positions do not treat their students as individuals, then this negative mindset will most likely lead to a lack of respect for students and authoritarian treatment that can lead to public criticism.

To push a student to a higher level of ability, the teacher should create a situation of emotional conflict so that the student can learn how to overcome it. High graded practitioners should push juniors out of their comfort zones to test their limits and challenge them to surpass themselves. The problem is that often there is only a fine line between what is appropriate and inappropriate in terms of training content, and occasionally individuals may lose control of their emotions. There are no definite solutions when dealing with the very subjective and personal topic of mental cultivation. We can say for certain, however, that people's minds are cultivated through endurance and from not avoiding conflict and harsh treatment. I believe that providing students with a training environment where they can experience and learn to deal with emotional conflict is the best solution.

So far in this instalment I have described how children need an environment where they are praised and appreciated in order to develop and grow. Next I stressed the importance of experiencing challenging new environments to develop their independence and self-esteem in late childhood to early adolescence. Environments focusing too much on denial or competition with others may lead to distrust of others and a sense of failure when not successful, which can result in children and teenagers quitting kendo. I also stressed the importance of having their perceived mental limits challenged and I believe it is an essential requirement in developing their minds in later adolescence. Valuing the dignity of the individual does not mean approving of youth as they are; we should challenge them with arduous training as this demonstrates a belief in their potential. The teacher-student relationship and senior-junior hierarchy should not be written off as old-fashioned and unnecessary; they are vital institutions that need to be preserved. Let us keep in mind the maxims "*shi-tei-dō-gyō*" (teacher and student walk the same path), and "*ji-ta-dō-kon*" (we all start out in the same place).

Establishing training values in accordance with the principle of *ji-ri-itchi*

The term "*itchi*" is often used in kendo, as in "*ki-ken-tai-itchi*" (spirit, sword, and body as one), "*shin-ki-ryoku-itchi*" (mind, spirit, and power as one), and "*ken-tai-itchi*" (combining offence and defence as one). Many of these maxims stem from the Eastern concept of "*shin-shin-itchi-gen*, which means "the mind and body are one and the same". Exploring these principles can lead us to discover the deeper meaning of kendo and help us cultivate ourselves. In simple terms, the concept of *shin-shin-itchi-gen* reminds us that we must obtain a high level of mind-body harmony to ensure victory when we are confronted by an opponent: this is the ultimate task of kendo training. This is also why the pursuit of techniques must involve cultivation of the mind. From the *nyūmon-ki* stage right through to the *jukuren-ki* stage, one must continually try to seek harmony of mind and body. This harmony allows us to further develop our character. Therefore, whilst teaching, we need to ensure that our students are aware of their own states of mind by not purely focusing on the pursuit of physical techniques. This will only result in producing competitors who lack personal integrity or character. "*Ji-ri-itchi*" (the unification of technique and theory) is another maxim that relates to attitudes in training that deserves thorough consideration. Much mental contemplation and physical practice is required to achieve this unification of physical motion and theoretical logic. Both aspects complement each other like wheels of a cart, but I wonder how many practitioners keep this in mind when training. I am deeply concerned that an increasing number of practitioners only recognise a limited rationale of the larger kendo whole. I cannot help feeling that the cultivation of the mind is being neglected at the expense of training to have better timing, speed, balance and power than one's training partners. I also feel that many practitioners, especially those in the introductory stages, misunderstand *ji-ri-itchi* and concentrate simply on performing rational and effective techniques when they should actually be building up a strong technical and theoretical foundation.

At an early stage of training, practitioners are experiencing rapid changes to their mental and physical functions, so it can often be difficult to foster attitudes to training or expect students to be cultivating their personalities as well. We can often see specific consequences of this problem in the *shiai* of children and teenagers, such as entering the *uchi-ma* without being mentally ready, making overly-defensive postures out of habit, sliding into *tsuba-zeriai* to avoid being struck, and interfering with their opponent's movements in *tsuba-zeriai* rather than trying to create their own opportunities to attack. The original aesthetic ideal of kendo was to stifle an opponent's moves and win with one clean attack. This ideal seems to have been replaced with the notion that one must block and defend against any potential attack. This results in low-quality kendo that even *shodan* to 3-dan grading candidates are not usually guilty of in their *tachi-ai*; it is mostly seen in competition where cunning defensive techniques are seen as an acceptable means to win. To overcome this situation there has been much discussion and attempts to gain greater consensus about the application of regulations when refereeing matches. These efforts appear to have had no discernible effect so far. On the contrary, we are starting to see more cunning moves and strategies that are not necessarily prohibited in themselves, but take advantage of ambiguity in the rules and perplex the referees involved. Every time I referee now, I find myself having to be stricter and stricter in my enforcement of competition regulations and guidelines for *yūkō-datotsu* and the cautioning of actions that may go against the rules.

There is a limit, however, to how much we can improve the quality of kendo simply by updating *shiai* and refereeing regulations. As a priority, I think standardised improvements should be made to teaching content and methodology. Teachers should evaluate each student's techniques and have them appreciate the aesthetic of pursuing one beautiful and decisive strike rather than haphazardly attacking with a flurry of techniques. If a strike does not first involve preparing oneself and overcoming the opponent's *kisei*, then it is just a casual strike and luck will be the only factor in it landing successfully. Teachers must encourage their students to examine their own strikes and see if they are suppressing their opponent's actions, attacking with strong determination, and completing their attacks with proper *zanshin*. This process of self-examination and reflection is an important undertaking for young people and to make a habit of it in training is also very important for character building. Having students consider the concept of *ji-ri-itchi* can help cultivate their minds through their pursuit of technique.

The following questions are excellent food for thought for young kendo students:

- What is kendo?
- Why should we bow when we enter a dojo?
- What is the significance of wearing a *dōgi* and *hakama*?
- What is the *shinai*?
- Why should we train hard in *kihon-geiko*?
- Why are *uchikomi-geiko* and *kakari-geiko* important?
- What is the real significance of *yūkō-datotsu*?
- When and why are we successfully struck by an opponent?
- How does kendo connect with our lives outside the dojo?

We can stimulate the minds of students with these questions, but it is pointless if they are participating in training thoughtlessly, are poorly motivated, or are participating against their will. Their characters will only be cultivated if they have a proactive and purposeful mindset and are training on their own initiative.

Building the correct foundations of technique through an emphasis on learning *kata*

Kata are a series of templates that provide us with base postures, shapes, forms, and actions, and encourage us to learn the movements that kendo originated from. Kendo could be described as a mould in which we pour ourselves to forge our mind and body. We must follow the shape of these *kata* templates and the kendo mould when we are in the initial stages of our training (the *shu* level of *shu-ha-ri*).

In my work as a university P.E. teacher, I included Bokutō ni Yoru Kendō Kihon-waza Keiko-hō in a practical class teaching kendo to beginners. As I had previously taught beginners by having them actually strike *bōgu*-wearing *motodachi* with *shinai*, I was able to compare and contrast the students' reactions and learning patterns in both scenarios. I discovered that some students showed resistance and fear of physically striking someone, while those who began with the *bokutō* patterns were able to calmly learn the underlying principles of *reihō* (etiquette), *shinpō* (the integration of their heart and mind), *tōhō* (sword-handling skills), and *shinhō* (body movements). Even if a beginner experiences a lot of *kihon-geiko* and *waza-geiko* with a *shinai*, it is still difficult for them to understand how to successfully strike a *motodachi* in *gokaku-geiko*. I was worried that they would be disheartened when they could not understand what warranted a successful strike and would have to accept decisions of win and loss at face value. In learning the *bokutō* patterns, on the other hand, I found that students paid attention to how they wore their *kendō-gi* and *hakama* and diligently practised the preset manners, skills and forms of the set. Students were able to gauge their progress clearly as improvements are more noticeable than when using a *shinai*. In basic practice with a *shinai*, students have a nervous tendency to try and compete against one another, but in the *bokutō* patterns there is a sense of cooperation and calmness and any tension or nerves are shared equally with their partners. Students will be quite busy learning the physical movements of the *bokutō* patterns, but at the same time they need to learn mental and interpersonal skills such as *aiki* (synchronising with their partner's spirit), *ki-atari* (pressuring), *kihaku* (displaying strong spirit), and *ifū* (creating an imposing presence). If a teacher simply has students focus on the physical movements, then they run the risk of losing students' attention, whereas, if the teacher stresses these mental and interpersonal aspects, then students are more likely to become curious about what it would be like to put on *bōgu* and try striking a partner for real.

Once beginners start learning *kata* as a foundation for their kendo skills, instructors must continually remind students that these underlying principles form the foundation of kendo and, no matter how much they progress, these principles will always be present in their training. This stage is also a valuable opportunity to study various kendo precepts before moving into regular kendo using a *shinai*. If teachers permit new students who are interested in competition to simply haphazardly learn random attack and defence motions without a basis in *kata*, then students may only be exposed to perhaps half of the principles and precepts that kendo is comprised of. I gained the aforementioned insights through teaching 15-lesson kendo modules to university students. However, even in this short period of time, I discovered some clues that may improve the *shiai* skills of some young practitioners whose performances

often stray from the principles of kendo. I would like to see more time invested in the training of the Nippon Kendo Kata and Bokutō ni Yoru Kendō Kihon-waza Keiko-hō than I am currently witnessing. I would also like to see more training in foundation practices such as *uchikomi-geiko*, *kirikaeshi*, and *kakari-geiko* with senior *motodachi* rather than focusing on practitioners squaring off against others of equal or similar skill.

I also believe that the number of competitions should be reduced as much as possible. The thrill of competition may entice many young practitioners to start training, but the sense of fulfilment obtained from fully committing to a hard *uchikomi-geiko* session will cultivate their minds and make more of a contribution to their character than competing will. Cultivating patience through interpersonal contact will strengthen the wills of young practitioners. If an individual focuses on *shiai* too much while they are young, they run the risk of losing interest in kendo as a lifelong pursuit. Training in kendo promotes an active and energetic mind that vitalizes us in our youth and supports our health in advanced age. Overly focusing on *shiai* can potentially rob us of this benefit. It is the duty of teachers to make their students aware as early in their kendo careers as possible that the essence of training is the pursuit of "beautiful strikes" and that we should not depart from this principle.

What do we gain from *keiko*?

I will now discuss what we should ideally obtain from kendo practice with reference to my early kendo years and certain events that relate to some of the aforementioned issues.

I started kendo when I was 10 years old. I practised once a week, and two instances stand out in my mind. The first was when I was performing *gokaku-geiko* in front of my teacher. I had been struck several times but I managed to instinctively make a good *kote-nuki-men* strike. My teacher stopped us immediately and praised my technique. The second instance was during a *shiai* in *kan-geiko* (winter training). As my teacher was refereeing my match he turned to the other children and said, "Look at how Sumi is holding his *shinai* with his right hand! He's holding it softly with a light grip! Look carefully!" Although I lost that *shiai*, I was very happy and proudly announced this to my parents when I got home. Even though I had a comparatively good physique as a child, I was not that athletic, and looking back now I can see that my teacher's warm praise was probably intended to encourage me because of this fact.

I did not have a proper teacher when I was in junior high school, but I remember practising *okuri-ashi* and *fumi-komi* around the dojo at the request of the senior students while they practised. Later, after having become a senior student myself, I visited another dojo and the teacher there praised my footwork. I think that I was able to keep my balance throughout *uchikomi* and *kakari-geiko* thanks to that footwork practice that my seniors had me do.

At the age of 15 I was invited to practise *iai* and I began learning Eishin-ryū with a *bokutō*. After some time I was presented with a real sword by a teacher who was a professional sword polisher. I still remember how impressed I was by the sharp and beautifully polished blade and how proud I felt when I carried the sword on my back to bicycle through town to the dojo. I also remember how guilty I felt when I tested the sword by cutting a branch off a tree in my garden. My *iai* teacher noticed the slight damage to the blade and reprimanded me strongly: "Do you want me to kick you out of this dojo?! A *katana* is not for you to go around cutting things with! It is for cutting down evil thoughts that arise in yourself!" When I joined the high school kendo club I devoted myself to kendo and stopped practising *iai*, but my body remembered the feeling of cutting the air with correct *hasuji*, drawing the sword from its scabbard, and re-sheathing it, which benefited both my *keiko* and *kata* training.

During the April-July term of my first year at high school, all I was allowed to do was *suburi* while I watched seniors practise *keiko*. After some time I was allowed to do *kirikaeshi*, *uchikomi-geiko* and *kakari-geiko*, and I became more proficient at making large men strikes. The continual repetition of basic techniques was hard and tiring, but the warm encouragement from seniors kept me going, as did the solidarity I felt with the other first year students practising in the same manner. In my last year at high school I took part in some competitions as one of the regular team members, but I do not remember winning at all. Even so, I presented myself for *keiko* with my teacher every day and was constantly pushed to the point of breathless exhaustion. My teacher praised my large men strikes and I turned these compliments into confidence. Despite our lack of technical prowess, the *motodachi* received our attacks and coached us until we were completely exhausted: "Come on! You're getting better!", "Once more!", "Use your left foot more!", "Don't throw your head back when you strike!", "Keep your posture straight!", and "Don't forget *tenouchi*!" The *motodachi* were not just allowing us to strike, but soliciting our best strikes through skilful distancing and positioning. We had no time to stop and catch our breath and we attacked the *motodachi* like this every day. The comment "Good work! Keep it up!" signalled the end of the exchange with each teacher. I was too exhausted to be thinking cognitively about my attacks but my body remembered the paces that they put us through.

When I joined the university kendo club, Yoshitomi-sensei one day said to me, "You've had enough basic striking practice, so now you need to learn how to *seme* using your *ki*", and he allowed me opportunities to practise *ji-geiko* with him. Even though I tried to *seme* him as much as I could, he continually foiled my *men* attacks with *de-gote* and *kaeshi-dō*, and his *kensen* was at my throat even when I thought that I had found an opening. Basically, our *ji-geiko* would turn into *uchikomi-geiko* partway though. One day, however, when I was fighting in a competition in my final year at university, I pressured my opponent with strong *seme* and he stepped back out of the *shiai-jō* even though I had made no motion to hit him at all. This made me realise what Yoshitomi-sensei had been talking about, and I was very excited and felt grateful to my teacher and opponent.

Now that I am a university teacher myself, I try to emulate this teaching style with my kendo students when receiving *uchikomi-geiko* and *kakari-geiko*. However, at first I found it difficult to provide them with appropriate distance, demonstrate *kisei* (spirit) to them, and verbally encourage them. I was also greatly concerned at how to encourage them to have a spirit of *sutemi* in their techniques in the few minutes of *ji-geiko* that I have with each student. I found myself learning a lot from *ji-geiko* with my students and I wondered if I was benefiting more than they were! Each encounter provided me with a great deal of food for thought. Some students commented that even though they are aware of me launching an attack, they sometimes find themselves frozen and cannot respond to the attack appropriately. These experiences led me to correct my attitude when doing *keiko* and to train with a slightly higher sense of *kigurai* than each student.

Over the years there have been countless times when higher grade seniors and other practitioners have observed me acting as *motodachi*. I find myself under particular scrutiny from people waiting in line for *ji-geiko* with me. No matter who is observing my *keiko*, I try to practise in a manner consistent with my age and grade. Being observed by so many people can be a valuable learning opportunity.

If your mind is unsettled or you are conceited or impatient, your *keiko* will be negatively influenced and this will carry over to your partner as well, who may feel unpleasant about doing *keiko* with you. I may be able to strike a lower grade practitioner, but of course, I also get struck by opponents who make a wholehearted or skilful attack. Being struck is unavoidable, so you should not let it affect your *kigurai*. If you maintain your *kigurai*, your partner hopefully will notice and appreciate this and you will be able to say *"Arigatō gozaimashita"* (Thank you very much) to each other with a genuine feeling of gratitude.

I am sure that all practitioners have felt the wonderfulness of kendo through similar or different experiences to those that I have described here. We are able to lead more fulfilling lives through helping each other to reach our goals. I feel a debt of gratitude to kendo for having provided me with direction in my life and a means to cultivate myself. I am so happy that I have spent my years practising kendo.

FILM REVIEW

By Michael Ishimatsu-Prime/Photos courtesy of Eleven Arts

UZUMASA LIMELIGHT

Eleven Arts, Japan, 2013
103 minutes

Director: Ken Ochiai
Screenwriter: Ono Hiroyuki
Producers: Mori Ko, Ono Hiroyuki, Sano Shohei
Starring: Fukumoto Seizō, Yamamoto Chihiro, Honda Hirotaro, Goda Masashi, Mine Rantaro, Kurizuka Asahi, Manda Hisako, Kobayashi Nenji, Matsukata Hiroki, Kinoshita Michihiro

Fukumoto Seizō, 71, is a true veteran of Japanese TV and cinema, appearing in hundreds of productions. Probably most familiar to non-Japanese audiences for his role as the "Silent Samurai" in the 2003 Hollywood film *The Last Samurai*, Fukumoto is not exactly what you would call a "leading man". He does, however, have a speciality that has kept him gainfully employed since he entered Kyoto's Toei Studios in 1958 at the age of 15. Fukumoto is a *kirare-yaku*, an actor/stuntman whose job it is to lose swordfights and die horribly in *jidai-geki* and *chambara* films and TV shows. After a career spanning 56 years, Fukumoto, known as "The Man who has been Killed 50,000 Times", has landed his first starring role in *Uzumasa Limelight*.

Set in Uzumasa, Kyoto, the mecca of *jidai-geki*, *Uzumasa Limelight* follows Kamiyama, an aging *kirare-yaku* played by Fukumoto, who struggles to find work after *Edo-Zakura* (Cherry Blossoms of Edo), the *jidai-geiki* TV show that has been his home for the last 40 years, is cancelled by the new studio head, who wishes to revamp the studio's content to make it more appealing to a younger audience. Held in high esteem by his peers as a great *kirare-yaku*, Kamiyama finds himself playing a *yakuza* corpse in a TV series, which does not go well, and then is employed in the studio's theme park putting on sword-fighting displays. Due to his age, he finds it increasingly difficult to get work, as do many of the other older *kirare-yaku* who do not have the right look for modern TV dramas.

Kamiyama then meets Satsuki (Yamamoto Chihiro), a young actress who wishes to learn the art of *kirare-yaku*. He takes her under his wing and coaches her as she lands a role on "Oda Nobu", a new TV series aimed at a young audience that focuses on the early life of warlord Oda Nobunaga. Symptomatic of the *jidai-geki* genre these days, the character of the young Nobunaga is played by a pop star, who is handsome, creepy and stupid in equal measure. "Why do I have to wear a wig to look bald?" he contends as the make-up artist tries to put a *chonmage* (samurai top-knot) hair-piece on him. The decision is also made to get the actors to use short green swords, as the blades can be added in post-production.

Director Ken Ochiai, who was raised in Japan but attended film school in the U.S., says that *Uzumasa Limelight* is a reflection of the current circumstances of *jidai-geki* and *chambara* film production in Japan.

"There used to be about 400-500 samurai movies made

a year, but now there are only about 10 in a good year, and in Tokyo, there are almost none. Most of them are shot in Kyoto because that is where the people who have the skills that are needed to make them are based. It is very difficult because the casting and art departments in Tokyo don't have the knowledge or props."

In *Uzumasa Limelight* the *kirare-yaku* are either very young or in their 50s and 60s or older, not their 30s or 40s. Again, Ochiai said that this is indicative of the conditions of the genre today. Based at Toei Studios in Kyoto, the Tsurugi-kai (The Sword Society) consists of actors whose speciality is sword fighting, and at present it has only about 15-20 members. There are some young actors that want to join the group, but ultimately they are not able to make a living with that type of work.

This sentiment is echoed by Fukumoto, who Ochiai says the film is loosely based on.

"The situation is as dire as you saw in the film, but we are hoping that the genre will make a comeback at some point. For now, I see it as my duty to help to teach the younger, new generation the skills I have learned over the years."

Fukumoto actually has had no formal training in kendo or other martial arts but began to learn his craft when he entered Toei Studios.

"I had no experience of martial arts, when I entered this business. I simply joined Toei as an employee. I learned everything from scratch from my seniors; how to kill people, how to be killed, how to fall. I had to practise in my dormitory falling down on my futon. Over the years I watched my comrades doing what they do and I had a chance to learn from them."

This is in stark contrast to 17-year-old Yamamoto Chihiro, who, in her feature film debut, plays Iga Satsuki, Kamiyama's protégée. Yamamoto began studying *tai-chi* at the age of three, and in 2012 won the gold medal for *sōjutsu* and silver medals for *kenjutsu* and *Chang quan* at the 4th World Junior Wushu Championships as well as gold in the *sōjutsu*, *kenjutsu*, and *Chang quan* events at the 2010, 2011, and 2012 JOC Junior Olympic Cups.

At its heart and in reality, *Uzumasa Limelight* is about passing the baton to a younger generation. Just as Fukumoto and Kamiyama are nearing the end of their careers, Yamamoto and Satsuki are beginning theirs. This changing of the guard is something that *Uzumasa Limelight*'s makers and stars hope to do: attract a new, younger audience to *jidai-geki* to keep its history and traditions alive.

Without being mean-spirited, *Uzumasa Limelight* pokes fun at *jidai-geki* and the situation in which it currently finds itself. It is, however, affectionate and reverential to the talent and films of the long-gone heyday of the genre. And, like Charlie Chaplin's Calvero in *Limelight* (1952), which this film also references, hence the name, it gives both Fukumoto Seizō and his character Kamiyama their moment in the "limelight".

Uzumasa Limelight had its Japanese nationwide release on July 12, 2014, and will be screening at various international film festivals around the world.

HISTORICAL ODDITIES

The Works of Tetsuya Noguchi

By Jeff Broderick

"I think there's no limit to what you can do by yourself in your own room. The most important thing is to follow your passion."

Positive Contact; 2011; H=95cm

In March 2014, Tokyo's Nerima Ward Museum of Art was transformed into another world by the work of Tetsuya Noguchi, whose strange yet familiar samurai figures, rooted in history while being somehow outside of time, evoke subtly mixed emotions.

Stepping from a sunny afternoon into the exhibit, called "A Field Guide to Warrior Species," the eyes take time to adjust. In the hushed atmosphere, the first figure, approximately half life-size, is so realistic that it prompts a double-take. A samurai, dressed in meticulously reconstructed armour, shades his eyes from the overhead spotlight. On the metal disk of his *maedate*—the ornamental crest at the front of his *kabuto* (helmet)—is the perforated greeting "*Yoroshiku*", or "Nice to meet you."

The temptation is to laugh, yet the undeniable elegance of the human figure and the warlike practicality of the armour makes me pause.

Next, a scroll, convincingly painted to appear hundreds of years old, portrays a frail-looking samurai boy seated in armour, but wearing anachronistic eyeglasses. The title is "Portrait of the Artist, Age 4." I want to laugh at the conceit, but there is something in the expression of the boy—a confidence, a certain precociousness—that makes me look deeper. Like the Mona Lisa, the expression hints at an underlying mystery.

Further along, another scroll depicts a proud, white-bearded warrior in bright-red armour, mounted atop an antlered horse. A red conical helmet adorns his head; his crest, a single pine tree. The title: "Santa Claus Samurai."

The works of Tetsuya Noguchi may appear silly or tongue-in-cheek at first glance, but like the dreamy works of surrealists like Dali or Magritte, they seem to tap into the viewer's subconscious to take on a deeper meaning. That the figures have captured people's imaginations is clear: this month-long exhibit drew more than 20,000 visitors, setting a new record for the venue.

Tetsuya Noguchi was born in Kagawa prefecture in 1980, on the island of Shikoku, and was always drawn to creating art. "Unlike other children who played soccer and did things outside, I just drew pictures and made models", he said. Noguchi's early obsessions were with picture books of dinosaurs and fossils, beetles and insects, robots, and the bizarre *kaiju* monsters that did battle with TV's Ultraman. He was fascinated by the special effects models in sci-fi films like *Star Wars*, and from a young age, he had a love for history, and in particular, samurai helmets and armour.

"When it came time for me to go to university, I had no intention of entering a company and working. I wanted to go to art school and keep drawing and creating. Actually, there was nothing else I was capable of doing", he admitted.

Noguchi began his art studies at Hiroshima University, majoring in oil painting, but he soon felt that something was lacking: "I found myself wondering if I could create artwork that I myself could enjoy. On one hand, I loved history, but I was also grateful to have all the blessings of modern life, like movies. I thought, why not try to create artwork where the lines between past and present have been taken away?"

This blurring of past and present is sometimes subtle, as with the figure of a young *ashigaru* foot soldier wearing a messenger bag and green sneakers that seem not at all incongruous with his brightly laced armour. Another figure of an older samurai carries a briefcase as he looks

Un Samouraï Vient; 2012, H=31cm

Insectman; 2012; 9 x 12cm each

up intently. It is the exact pose I have seen a hundred salarymen strike as they study an electronic signboard on a train platform. Another old warrior appears to be transported away, listening to music on a pair of headphones that sport the crest of the Tokugawa shogun.

Other work is more obviously fanciful, like the full-size armour made for a housecat, or the samurai flying with a helicopter assembly emerging from his helmet like Doraemon's *take-copter* (or if you prefer, Inspector Gadget). Elsewhere, a samurai streaks across the sky with an iron rocket pack strapped to his back. Silly? Perhaps, but I also could not help but think of the kamikaze pilots of World War II.

I asked Noguchi: did he see his figures as travellers from the past? Or are they inhabitants of some mysterious, alternate universe? "I think the best thing I can do is to create people that are neither from the past nor the present—just a universal image of human beings. I'm pleased if people feel they are mysterious."

A number of young artists in Japan—among them Akira Yamamoto and Hisashi Tenmyoya—have achieved recognition by mixing traditional motifs and classical

Daremo Shabette ha Ikenai
[No one may speak]
2008; H=32cm

styles with modern themes. But Noguchi does not feel that this is a movement or a trend, so much as a generational issue. "I'd like to think that my artwork is actually contributing to providing relevance to the next generation to receive the culture from past generations."

What role does the culture of bygone times play for people today? "Well, everyone knows that dinosaurs have disappeared, but actually, if you look around our modern world, traces of the dinosaurs remain everywhere, just in different forms. For example, dinosaurs changed their forms to birds. So from my perspective, Japanese culture tends to take on the form of previous culture while changing its form naturally."

One striking aspect of Noguchi's work is the ambiguity of his creations' expressions. Some figures appear to be deep in contemplation. Others seem tired, or sad. Absent are the heroic poses usually associated with the samurai. Instead, some of Noguchi's samurai figures are curled up in a fetal position and mounted in specimen boxes.

"I had a strong purpose of trying to connect [my work] to animals and biological specimens, because for me, samurai are not something to be admired as heroes, but rather something that should be researched in order to be understood. For example, when someone wants to know about sharks, no matter how much one looks at them and thinks about them, they won't come any closer to understanding what they are really about. If you want to know about sharks in real situations, you have to study and conduct research." Does Noguchi believe the samurai are so separated from us by history that they are almost another species?

"Actually, I believe they were the same as us. For example, although the societal rules of the samurai were completely different than ours today, on a basic level, samurai were the same as modern people… Different situations and environments, but the same humanity."

Noguchi faithfully recreates traditional construction techniques with modern materials like acrylic paints, plastics and resins. Fabric is painstakingly stitched by hand. Tiny plates of armour are lacquered and laced together with string. Even the figures' facial hair and eyebrows are inserted strand by strand. The process of creating a 30-cm figure takes around two months; larger figures can take much longer.

The historical accuracy and research surrounding each piece is also amazing; Noguchi's studio is filled with reference materials. "I am often asked if I belong to armour or historical research groups. I don't—I actually learned everything on my own. I think there's no limit to what you can do by yourself in your own room. The most important thing is to follow your passion."

Chanel Samurai, Seated in Armour
2009; 86 x 41cm

Target Marks 1580 - 1610
2009; H=94cm and H=96 cm

BOOK REVIEW

"Alex Bennett has produced the first truly authoritative translation and analysis of Hagakure—perhaps the most famous text ever written about samurai honor—to appear in any Western language. Simultaneously erudite and accessible, this volume belongs on the bookshelves of anyone—scholar or hobbyist alike—interested in samurai culture, or modern perceptions thereof."

— Dr. Karl F. Friday, author of *Samurai, Warfare and the State in Early Medieval Japan* and *Japan Emerging: Premodern History to 1850*

"[Alex Bennett] is the very best writer on martial arts alive today and [his] work needs to be showcased to the general public."

— Don Warrener, President, *Budo International*

"Dr. Bennett possesses a profound knowledge of, and deep insight into, the world of Japanese bushido. This expertise has been enhanced by his extensive practical experience of the traditional martial arts of Japan, and his proficiency in this domain is highly acclaimed."

— Tetsuo Yamaori, former Director of the International Research Center for Japanese Studies

"[A] strong point is a scholarly and succinct introduction that grounds the work in historical and social context, equipping the reader with a cultural map of Yamamoto's world. Footnotes provide valuable background and add resonance throughout, keeping names and familial relations straight, highlighting pertinent cross-references and generally rendering the work accessible to contemporary readers."

— *The Japan Times*

Search for "Bennett" and "Hagakure" on Amazon.com

常識を超える
勝利のゴールドマーク

ALL JAPAN BUDOGU
FREE INTERNATIONAL SHIPPING ON ALL ORDERS!

www.alljapanbudogu.com

The 'All Japan Pitch©' brand is a registered trademark ©2014 株式会社全日本武道具センター

Shinai Sagas
The Champion

By Charlie Kondek

Word had been passed, in the dojo and in the restaurants, as announcement or aside, by e-mail, text and Facebook, that the Champion would return to the United States, that he would attend a seminar at Mokkei Dojo on one of the stops in his tour of several American cities. It was the subject of much curiosity and discussion. Some of the younger Americans knew the name, of course, given their increasing familiarity with competitive kendoka, but they held for him the same reverence they would hold for any such high level person visiting their soil. Yes, they knew he was multiple times a champion, but what was so significant about him? Why were eyebrows raised and lips pursed when he was spoken of?

The Japanese that knew him better tried to explain in English. Ando said, "There are not many on his level. Everyone agrees there is something special about his kendo". Wada said, "He is not my favourite player, maybe, or the one I admire most, but, how can I say? He can be a model for our kendo". A thought. "Especially our competition kendo."

It was left to Swan to interpret. He mused on the topic one night when Nygaard's crowd visited and the beer had made him thoughtful. "I first saw him several years ago on a return visit to Japan when I was lucky enough to catch the All Japans on TV in a pub. No one really suspected what he was capable of back then – I mean they didn't know he would go on to be one of a handful of people to win it as many times as he has. That's part of it, that's the big part of it. But, the other part of it is he's getting to that age where he won't be able to stay competitive much longer. These younger guys are gonna overtake him. And everyone wonders if or how his style is going to adjust under the pressure."

"What about his style?" interjected Mazurski. "What style is that?"

"Calm," Swan said. "An unflappable calm. That's the thing I think so many people admire. When the pressure in a match has built and built and other people are falling apart, he's still got it together, retaining the same placid exterior. That's what it is."

Pavel broke in. "It's also the thing that people are bothered about. When he doesn't win, it looks like he isn't trying hard enough. Like he can't be bothered unless all the right elements are there."

"And yet," Swan said, "and yet, he is on a short list of kenshi to have done what he's done. To have won it as often as he has."

"What do you think he's like?" asked Skenazy.

"We're gonna find out," said Nygaard.

"He has come to the U.S. before," said Swan. "I was here the last time. It'll be interesting to see how he has changed." He scratched his chin idly. "If he's changed."

On the day of the seminar there were so many people moving around in the gym, greeting one another, adjusting equipment, seeing to the myriad details of transportation and attendance, that at first the Champion was not noticed. He was just another Japanese face in the crowd, a little taller perhaps, a little more possessed and regal. But then the attendees began to be aware of the Champion. He had a quiet demeanour, and yet he radiated action; either his bearing or the *nafuda* that bore his name in English and his country, "Japan", caused a slight eddying in the crowd of people preparing for the seminar, created space around him. And though he smiled, and nodded, and spoke in short, quiet, friendly words to everyone he encountered, no one got too close to him, not the Japanese, who spoke his language, nor the North Americans, for whom he had a small vocabulary, not even the organisers of the seminar, Honda-sensei and Ogawara-sensei himself. The Champion seemed part of the crowd but apart from it.

"And now I would like, to introduce to you, our distinguished, guest, from Japan." The words in English came haltingly from Ogawara's tongue as he introduced the Champion, his credentials, and something of his history. The Champion smiled warmly as he addressed the assembly, which consisted of more than a hundred attendees from dojo in four surrounding U.S. states and parts of Canada. "I watched you warm up," the Champion said through a microphone and amplifier, his words in Japanese translated into English by Sato-sensei. "I would like to offer you some feedback on the best way to make *kamae* and practise *suburi*."

In the days and weeks that followed the seminar the attendees compared their experiences and what they had learned. Any visiting sensei leading a seminar has only a short time to devote to a handful of subjects, they agreed, and some of the more experienced or insightful ones pointed out that the seminar leader must also "read the room", a very big room in most cases, and adjust his teaching to the skill level and composition of the participants. "Most of these sensei fall back on giving a very orthodox lesson in fundamentals," Swan remarked.

"Especially when they come to the U.S.," Nygaard opined, a hint of cheek in his words.

The Champion certainly did this, too, but he was also eager to show something of his own self, of his own style, in what he imparted. "On the one hand, yes, it was pretty conventional," Mazurski noted, "some of the stuff he taught. But on the other hand he also talked a lot about his own experiences and his own approach to things."

"I don't think I heard anything I hadn't heard before," said Breckenridge. "But maybe the way he put things, that was unique." Among themselves, the Japanese picked up on smaller clues unknown to the non-Japanese speakers, turns of phrase that either indicated deeper meaning or pointed to the experienced, the learned.

As all expected, the Champion spoke of *rei*, of *kamae* and *suburi*. "*Suburi* is never just a warm up," the Champion said. "Every time you cut you have to imagine you are cutting the *men*, cutting from the top of the head to the chin."

"Now, I would like to focus on *kirikaeshi*. Please, get your *men* and *kote* and remember your places." The gym was large, but even so, they were so numerous that they had divided into two halves and in clusters of three at about the same skill level; only two of the three could perform each drill and then the third person would rotate in while another went out. They spent a lot of time on *kirikaeshi*, as expected. "This is what I am noticing," the Champion said through his interpreter, and then gave several remarks. Again the emphasis was on details, and also in making each cut in the series with the right intention. The Japanese noted a deep seriousness to this drill.

The Champion then focused the seminar on *waza*, and for many this was the most memorable portion. It was rare, many felt, to have a kenshi of such standing give attention to such specific tactics, to the details of taking *ippon* or winning a match, and this, it seemed to them, was what the Champion did. For example, he showed how one might draw an opponent forward and then take *kote*. Or to lower an opponent's hands by pressing down on his *shinai* and open *men*. Many of the attendees hungrily retained the details of these *waza*, while others tried to see in the way the Champion taught them glimpses into principles of attack. In either case, it was agreed, the Champion tried to fill these lessons with something of himself. "Here is a way I have found that has worked for me," he said. "At these times, you may be able to make the opponent move in this way. Then, you can make *ippon*."

And yet, Ando thought. He found it difficult to express in words what he was thinking, until much later, and then he was at first afraid to say what he was thinking.

Two things were evident every time the Champion demonstrated – his hands and his legs. His hands when he cut showed remarkable coordination and power, expert *tenouchi*. His legs showed an uncommon springiness, confidently covering a lot of floor in magnificent lunges. Many of the attendees remarked about it afterwards. "Did you see his legs?" Mazurski asked. "Unreal." "How many hours of practice", Wada wondered. "Maybe he was born to do this." Many said, "And he makes it look so effortless".

The Champion, with Ogawara-sensei and Honda-sensei helping him mind the time, reserved the last forty minutes of the seminar for *ji-geiko*. Instead of lines, Ogawara-sensei arranged the pairs so that almost everyone in the higher levels could have a one- to two-minute turn with the Champion. Even so, for many, after they had *keiko* with the Champion, they stopped to watch him fight instead of continuing with the next opponent, usually by mutual consent. The Champion displayed, as was to be expected, excellent fundamentals. But besides that he exhibited superior timing, and of course what to most was unimaginable endurance and patience. He did not set out to dismantle each opponent, but, in accordance with the proper way of conducting one's self in this situation, lowered his skill level to match each person, to a level of intensity that was just above, to produce for them an opponent capable of demonstrating an exemplary kind of kendo appropriate to their level. Many of the attendees, especially the young college Americans from Nygaard and Mazurski's club, tried to execute the *waza* the Champion had taught that evening, and this elicited a friendly nod from him when performed well. The Champion was not interested in winning, only, it seemed, in fundamentals, in coaxing from those lucky enough to have a try with him a good effort, something they could learn from. What wasn't on display, many noted later, was the style of fencing the Champion exhibited in the competitive matches with which they were familiar.

As the 40-minute period wound down, the most advanced attendees crossed swords with him. Now, the fighting from the other participants ceased altogether as everyone turned to watch the Champion take on the seminar's toughest members. Swan held *kamae* with him for a long time, probing, trying to pressure the Champion. When Swan forced *men*, the Champion met him with *men*; the Champion's was straight, Swan's wide of the mark. Ando launched a very fast *men* attack at the Champion that was batted down and countered. Trying for *kote*, the Champion instead executed a winning *kote-men*. Wada struck several times at the Champion. Each time his attacks were stymied. Then, when Wada hesitated, unsure of his next move, the Champion cut a large, popping *men* to Wada's right side.

Now Sato-sensei approached. There was much more tension as the *kensen* of each man circled. Sato attempted to force the Champion's hand by stepping in; both fencers' *shinai* collided in an indecisive *ai-men*. Again, Sato came for the Champion's *men*. A great, close *dō* cut swept across Sato with a resounding crack. Now the Champion took Sato's *kote*. Sato regrouped, and for the next several seconds they fought for position until time expired.

Most of the seminar's participants dropped into *seiza* to watch the final match between the Champion and Ogawara-sensei. As each rose from *sonkyo*, a silence fell over the large gym, broken only by the challenging *kiai* from Ogawara and the Champion's reply. There was a subtle play of *kensen*. The eyes of the more experienced onlookers were drawn to all the finer points of both combatants' *kamae*, the spread of the feet, the position and tension of the hands, the tip of the swords, the carriage of the head, the gaze and expression of the face. Ogawara's face where it was visible behind the *men* broadcast a fierceness such as many who knew him had never seen. The Champion now displayed the unnerving calm for which he was known. All who watched, regardless of their ability to see, felt the tension between them rise as their *kensen* probed and pressured, as their bodies shifted, a little forward, a little back. Now Ogawara-sensei began to boil the pot a little more; his *shinai* seemed to tremble and twitch, to test the Champion's steadiness, first on the *omote* and then the *ura* side. Ogawara inched forward. The Champion stepped back. Again, the elder sensei stepped forward, and now there was an explosion, a mutual exchange of *men* cuts in which both *shinai* were knocked astray, neither a decisive strike.

All in all, this happened two more times. Only three cuts were made in total, by each man. The rest of the time was spent in intense, pressured movement of the body and *shinai* as each sought to force open the other. All of the cuts were made mutually. None of them were decisive.

And then the seminar was finished and the rituals of ending were enacted, the lining up, the bows, the rounds of applause, the closing remarks, the seated bows in *zarei*, and words of appreciation. And of course, the group photos, from multiple cameras, multiple times. The seminar was followed by a banquet in a room at the back of a Chinese restaurant sequestered behind polished, wooden red rails. The Champion at the head table sat with most of the Japanese sensei from the host and visiting dojo, but also with a few Americans, including Swan and Nygaard. Others clustered together based on affiliation, or randomly; for many, it was one of three or four times that year they'd have an opportunity to chat in person. The buffet was simple and plentiful, the drinking somewhat restrained – indeed, for a kendo get-together the atmosphere was relaxed, as many of the attendees would have to return home by long drives, having only come in for the seminar and not a long weekend that also included a tournament and testing. Invisibly, the attendees of the banquet slimmed down until only perhaps a score clustered around the head table where the Champion, sitting comfortably in athletic wear beneath hanging scrolls depicting Chinese mountains, enjoyed the last of his meal. Some plates were cleared and fresh bottles of beer brought to the table. A bottle of *shōchū* and a bucket of ice materialized. Some were drinking tea. Mazurski was the one who said what many were thinking. Could they have "questions and answers" with the Champion, a not uncommon occurrence in their federation when someone so notable visited? The Champion, with the same demeanour of calm he had displayed all evening, the same patience and friendliness, was happy to oblige.

Ogawara himself started them off. How long had the Champion been practising kendo, at what age had he started? The Champion, speaking in Japanese, his remarks translated into English by Sato-sensei, said he had started at the age of eight. Someone asked what training was like through his school years. He said the teachers that supervised him as a child were very strict, that high school, though intense, took second place to studying, and that the college years had been the most difficult, with two practices a day and special camps. What about police training, someone else asked, what was that like? The Champion said it was constant, but that he was, after all, a policeman, and sometimes the training was overshadowed by his work. Still, he confessed, when he was preparing for competition, he had often been given special leave from his duties to do nothing but train for it. The Champion described some of his training methods during this period, which included extra practices at the police dojo but also visiting other dojo and solitary practice with footwork, *suburi*, and a striking dummy.

What else did the Champion do for physical fitness? Running, he said, especially sprints, and calisthenics, especially body weight exercises. Someone finally struck up the nerve: How can I get better at *shiai*? Everyone nodded and smiled. The Champion, too, smiled and gave this some thought. "Of course," he said, "by hard training in fundamentals, including *suburi*, *kirikaeshi*, *kakari-geiko*, *ji-geiko*. But also, by experience, by competing in *shiai*, every chance you get. You benefit from the experience.

Maybe..." he thought about his next words, cocking his head thoughtfully to one side in what seemed to many a characteristic Japanese manner. Maybe it was possible to practise *shiai-geiko* in one's everyday *ji-geiko*. Certainly, if one practised *ippon-shōbu*, one could or should approach it like *shiai*. But, also, the Champion thought, all kenshi should strive to make their *shiai* kendo exactly like their everyday kendo and exactly like their *shinsa*, their testing, kendo – all should be the same. "But," he added, "this I think is the ultimate goal of everyone and is very difficult to do." Anyway, *suburi*, *kirikaeshi*, *kakari-geiko*, *ji-geiko*, and competition itself were his suggestions for becoming stronger in competition kendo.

And what did the Champion "think of foreign kendo?" he was asked. The Champion said he admired it very much and it was very similar to what was practised in Japan. What was different about Japanese kendo and foreign kendo? Here the Champion struggled to express himself. The other Japanese kenshi seemed to nod in sympathy. For one thing, the Champion said, in Japan people are able to start kendo much younger, in a bigger community, with more experienced senpai and sensei, and to practise more often. But for another, there was a context to Japanese kendo, a cultural context – he and Sato-sensei and the other Japanese struggled to produce this word – the "context" was different. And, this was difficult to explain, though, he added, foreigners did their best to understand.

Do you study *iai* or *koryū* also? The Champion said he studied the Seitei Iai forms. And the old sensei, he was asked, what were some of their characteristics or habits? Here the Champion, and all the Japanese present, laughed. Of course they were very strict, he said. And obsessed with basics, with fundamentals. They were strict disciplinarians, they would push very hard. And they were notoriously hard drinkers. He laughed and said, in English, "Old boys". He said something to Ogawara-sensei privately and then added, "How can I say? This old generation were more complete in their skills. They practised kendo but also iaido and the old *koryū*, and *jūjutsu* and judo and the police techniques, and aikido. And they practised hard and drank hard and were very strict."

It had grown late. The Champion was fighting politely to stifle his yawns, still tired from jet lag and the change in time zones from Japan to the U.S. And it was evident to everyone that not only he but also his audience had grown tired. Someone sneaked in one more question: How did the Champion like his chances in this year's All Japan competition? The Champion only smiled shyly and said his opponents would be very strong but that he would do his best. Ogawara-sensei thanked the Champion for "questions and answers" and said it was time for them all to retire. Reluctantly, the company parted, first from the Champion, then from Ogawara and Sato and the other sensei, then, still saying their goodbyes in the parking lot, from each other.

In the weeks that followed the seminar, the various attendees, spread among four states and parts of Canada, reflected on and analysed their experience with the Champion. All agreed it had been a remarkable opportunity, something they would carry with them for years. Among Nygaard's crew, one night after practice, over beers at their usual place, Mazurski speculated: "It was almost like that Zen story about the cats." What? "The cats – there's this samurai with a rat in his house and he gets all these different cats to try to take out the rat. They can't, but then they find one ordinary-looking cat that can, and afterwards all the cats sit around asking the master cat how he is able to do what he does. It becomes a discourse on Zen. The whole thing sort of felt like that." Days later, Mazurski produced the text in a D.T. Suzuki book, and someone else found the Hellman translation. They pondered it. Yes, maybe that's what it was like, the master cat communicating some kind of core truths to the other cats, who could only grasp part of the concept, the complete concept of how to approach martial arts and life.

Swan afterward had thoughts he kept to himself for a while, then confessed privately to Pavel and Graham. He had a question he had not voiced during "questions and answers". His question was: How are you able to keep that unmoving calm under all that pressure? How are you able to keep it so that the other falls apart? He should have asked it, Pavel agreed – what was he afraid of? Being embarrassed? Swan thought of the old maxim about an unasked question, how asking a question risks looking like a fool for a while, but that not asking it risks remaining a fool for longer. Maybe he had missed an opportunity.

This was the talk among some of the non-Japanese. Among the Japanese, the talk was more guarded. They were more used to experiencing such greatness, had kept company, if not with champions of this man's calibre, sensei of great ability. They had perhaps more granular ideas about the man they encountered, but still, they found it difficult to share their thoughts about him until, at a candid moment as the tea cooled after a few Kirin had been put down with noodles, Ando shared what he had been thinking. "Maybe he has such great ability, is such a natural, that he finds it impossible to teach what he knows. He cannot teach what he knows – what he is able to do… he has a talent for it… it cannot be taught."

And what, Wada asked, about the Champion's suggestion that one's *shiai* kendo should be the same as one's everyday kendo and the same as one's *shinsa* kendo? "Well certainly that's the goal," Ando said. "Do you think… he is… close to that?" They all examined the kendo they had seen that day, the kendo he had tried to demonstrate. Some of them imagined the kendo they had seen the Champion perform in his many victories at the highest levels of competitive kendo. What was different about him?

It was with this inquiry, later that year, that each of them watched the All Japan Kendo Championships, on Japanese cable TV or streaming over the internet, eager to see how the Champion would perform, would win, eager to see inside the man's kendo. He did not make it to the semi-finals that year.

NAGINATA Monbushō Seitei Kata

By Baptiste Tavernier

Introduction

In 1941, the Dai-Nippon Butokukai published a set of generic *kata* and teaching guidelines entitled *Naginata-dō Kihon Dōsa* (see *Kendo World* issue 6.3) for the purpose of promoting a unified form of naginata to be taught in schools all around Japan. Naginata was adopted into the female physical education program in 1913 as an extracurricular activity, and then elevated to an elective subject from 1937. Until that time, naginata instruction in schools had always consisted of the study of *ryūha* techniques, mainly from the Tendō-ryū and the Jikishin Kage-ryū traditions, with no unified curriculum from one school or the other. Thus, the Butokukai's initiative gave momentum to the modernisation of the naginata education that would continue on throughout the war.

However, the *Naginata-dō Kihon Dōsa* failed to achieve its purpose because it was seen as a simplification of the Jikishin Kage-ryū, more than as a unification of different traditions, and above all else because it did not constitute a modern system in which a naginata exponent would face another naginata practitioner. Instead, it continued to promote the old pattern of a *naginata* facing a sword, which was inconvenient in a school curriculum because the students were required to become proficient in the use of two very different weapons in a short period of time.

A *naginata* versus *naginata* approach was to be devised the same year by Niino Kyūhei (*Nihon Kokumin Naginata-dō Kyōhon* — see *Kendo World* issue 6.4); his system consisted of basic strikes that could be used in *shiai* and easily combined in *kata*. In fact, he created a set of five patterns entitled "Naginata Dantai Taiteki no Kata" ("Naginata Kata in Formation Against the Enemy"), which resemble the forms currently practised in modern naginata. Although it was clearly a long-awaited evolution in terms of pedagogy, Niino Kyūhei's influence did not successfully disseminate beyond the borders of Shiga prefecture where he taught.

The last step in naginata's evolution during the war was finally made by Sakakida Yaeko, a Tendō-ryū exponent who was commissioned by the Ministry of Education (MOE) to create a new official *naginata* versus *naginata* system that would be used as a component of the *tairenka* (physical discipline) classes in Japan's schools. This method consisted of basic techniques and a set of seventeen *kata* that would later become known as the "Monbushō Seitei Kata" (hereinafter referred to as the "MSK").

The MSK has since fallen into obscurity; today, nearly all practitioners are unaware of its existence. Nevertheless, because it served as a basis for the inception of modern naginata's curriculum after the war, its relevance to the history and development of naginata should not be overlooked. A survey of the MSK may be conducted based on the guidelines that were officially released in 1944 by the MOE, and a report of a round-table discussion between Sakakida Yaeko and several officials from the MOE ("Naginata - Yōmoku no Seishin to Sono Shidō", published in *Gakuto Taiiku*, 1944). The guidelines were published in a series of three bulletins (one for primary education, one for high school and one for normal school), which detailed the *tairenka* classes' naginata curriculum for each grade. Those guidelines were produced in text only and did not feature any illustrations.

We recreated the seventeen patterns of the MSK based on what was described in the guidelines. Here, we must acknowledge that such a process cannot be deemed valid in most cases, because through text only the description of a *kata* may retain its sequences (for example: "strike to the head, then block, then final strike to the left shin"), but it inevitably fails to convey adequately many technical aspects (how should I strike the head, what is the direction of the blade when blocking, what is the whole body movement involved when striking the left shin?). Fortunately, however, regarding the MSK we know most of the technical syllabi upon which the *kata* were built:

— Sakakida Yaeko explained in the monthly magazine *Kendo Nihon* in 1982 that the *shikake-ōji* patterns practised currently in modern naginata were created based on the MSK. Indeed, both *kata* have similar moves and a few identical patterns. Modern naginata practitioners are therefore equipped with a base of knowledge of the MSK.
— Nevertheless, one can reasonably assume that some technical aspects may have changed when arranging the MSK in order to form the *shikake-ōji*. If one refers to the report of the round-table discussion between Sakakida and the Monbushō officials, one would see that several technical points have evolved from one *kata* to another. Dissimilarities and resemblances all appear in the report.
— Sakakida states in the report that whenever the *naginata* is moved, the whole body should move as well in unison; this fundamental concept has been preserved in *shikake-ōji*, and is well known by modern naginata exponents. Positions of the rear hand for each type of strike are also mentioned; they globally match those in *shikake-ōji*, with the exception of *tsuki*. The way of performing thrusts in the MSK is extremely peculiar, as it was copied exactly from the *jūken-jutsu* (bayonet) *tsuki*, with the rear hand reaching the solar plexus. This technique does not exist any longer in modern naginata.

Combining the knowledge we have of modern naginata, the indications that were left to us in the official guidelines and the round-table discussion, it is possible to recreate the MSK. There are nevertheless a few points that we cannot peremptorily ascertain. Firstly, there are scarce explanations on how to demonstrate *zanshin*, and

Sakakida Yaeko

only up to the fifth *kata*. Therefore, we decided in our reconstruction to adopt the modern way where *ōji* takes two steps back after the final attack, for every pattern. Secondly, there are no details of how to thrust with the *ishizuki*: should the thrust be done the same way it is performed in modern naginata or in the *jūken-jutsu* style? Thrusts with the *ishizuki* in the MSK are made to the lower abdomen, but attempts to perform the technique in the *jūken-jutsu* style have proven to be quite awkward. We therefore adopted the modern manner of execution for our reconstruction. Finally, there are no explanations regarding the *ishizuki* attacks to the head. However, as Sakakida Yaeko was a Tendō-ryū exponent, we can assume that those strikes in the MSK are done in the same basic manner as those particular to that *ryūha*.

The Monbushō Seitei Kata

The 1944 official guidelines for the *tairenka naginata* can be summarized as below:

<u>1 — Kihon (basics)</u>
The content of the guidelines' *kihon* section is entirely consistent with the modern naginata curriculum.

The only difference worth mentioning would be the *kirikaeshi* sequence, which then included two *tsuki* to the throat.
- *Reihō* (*tachi-rei*; *za-rei*).
- *Kamae* (*rittō* - now "*shizentai*"; *hōtō* - now "*mugamae*"; *chūdan*; *hassō*; *waki*; *gedan*; *jōdan*).
- Footwork.
- Cuts (single cuts, *nidan waza*, *sandan waza* and *renzoku waza*).
- *Kirikaeshi* (*tsuki*, *tsuki*, *sa-yū men* and *sa-yū sune*).

2 — Ōyō (advanced techniques)

The *ōyō* section is divided in three parts:
- Three "*harai* then strike" exercises (*harai-tsuki*, *harai-men*, *harai-sune*).
- Three "*degashira* then strike" exercises (*tsuki* while the opponent is assuming *hassō*; *men* while the opponent is assuming *waki*; *sune* while the opponent is swinging up (*furiage*) their *naginata*).
- The 17 attack/defence patterns that would later be known as the Monbushō Seitei Kata, and that served as a basis for the creation of modern *shikake-ōji*.

At the time of the official release in 1944, the MOE organised a round-table discussion with Sakakida Yaeko and several officials in order to further explain some aspects of the guidelines. Present were Sakuma Keizō (MOE - Bureau of Physical Education), Hayashida Toshisada and Tanaka Yoshio (Commissioners, Ministry of Education), Sakakida Yaeko (MOE - PE study committee), Ueshima Shizuko (teacher at Sakai Municipal Women's High School), Fujisaki Hiroyuki (Director, Tokyo Physical Education Department), and Ishibashi Fujino from the Tokyo Mukojima Western Public School.

The round-table starts with usual comments on Japanese history, martial arts and womanly virtues:

> [...] We built our nation by means of the art of war. During the 3,000 years of Japan's glorious history, our unshakeable people have been nurtured with the spirit of war. The spirit of militarism has become the flesh and blood of the people. [...] "Budo" means putting into practice this spirit of militarism. The Way of the Empire combined with militarism gives life to our traditional budo[...] It is crucial that our female students, as daughters of the Empire, cultivate a healthy body and a daring spirit, train their manners and their preparedness. Through naginata, our traditional female budo, students will forge themselves, polish a frigid and dignified spirit and cultivate womanly virtues.
>
> [...] However, nowadays, a *naginata* is a very rare weapon, and obviously nobody in the near future is going to fight battles using a real *naginata*. To put it simply, if we would have been thinking about a martial art that women could actually use, then we would rather have opted for *bōjutsu*, judo or *tanken-jutsu*... What made us choose naginata is the fact that naginata has been seen as the representative martial art for Japanese women.
>
> [...] We are at war, and we need the strength of motherhood in order to exalt the fighting spirit and morale of our officers and soldiers at the forefront. Thanks to those naginata guidelines, women, as subjects of the nation, will be able to polish a virtuous strength. As daughters of the Empire, they must train in those guidelines and embody them in their daily life. As wives and daughters of the samurai, they shall raise their readiness.

The MOE also advocates here the separation between state education and *ryūha*. This is still the case nowadays.

> [...] We have respect for all the *ryūha*, and it is important that we continue to hand down from now on and for ever the excellent spirit and techniques. However, [...] those guidelines do not follow exclusively a particular *ryūha*, neither are they a compilation of techniques coming from each different *ryūha*. [...] Our naginata is an original system that has been devised to fit our school education system. There is intention neither to unify the *ryūha*, nor to deny them. [...] To put it simply, naginata education in school, from now on, will specifically follow those guidelines, and we will thus ask each *ryūha* to continue promoting their art outside the school system.

Naginata's characteristics get standardised according to these numbers: for primary schools, the weapon shall be 6-*shaku* long (182cm), weight more than 750 grams and feature a blade of 42cm; from junior high school, 7-*shaku* (212cm), over 860 grams and with a 55cm blade. The guidelines promote outdoor training exclusively.

During the round-table discussion, Sakakida Yaeko gives detailed explanations of the technical aspects that form the basis of her new naginata system. As naginata practitioners will see, most of the technical syllabi she created still pertain to modern naginata:

> I think that if one practises *kihon* well enough, she will have no problem when moving on to *ōyō*.
> I strongly advocate to polish the basics first, especially *furiage men*. When women perform this technique, it

is soft and strong at the same time. But just swinging up your weapon is not enough; *tenouchi* and the *tai-no-hiraki* (the body facing sideways at the end of the strike) are of the outmost importance here. It has nothing to do with muscular strength; it is really crucial to stress that women should not use their arms' strength when they cut.

Women are frailer than men. But by building on this lack of muscular power, we can achieve tremendous things. Of course, men's budo is also based on softness rather than brute force, but this aspect is the very essence of women's budo and thus must be even more emphasised. These new guidelines insist, for each technique, on *tenouchi*, grip and *tai-no-hiraki*. Students must be aware of that. They will tend to disregard *tai-no-hiraki*, will cut with their body not facing completely sideways, and thus will not be able to use their strength to the fullest. In other words, the main objective of practising *kihon* is to be able to cut by using a full *tai-no-hiraki*. For example, when you perform a *furiage men*, you must do so facing the hips to the front, and only when you slash down should you be facing completely sideways again. This is *tai-no-hiraki*. At the very moment where you turn your hips (*tai-no-hiraki ma-yoko*), the energy of the blade is decreased. You do not need to use brute force, rotating your hips gives you enough strength to perform each and every strike. Also, correct *tenouchi* will make your techniques strong. However, it is important to note that even if one endeavours to be extremely strict about her *tai-no-hiraki*, it is crucial that she first polishes her *kamae*. *Kamae*, or posture, allows you to keep a replete spirit (*kihaku*).

Next, let us examine the position of the back hand when slashing. When performing a *sune* cut, *sayū men* cuts or *tsuki*, the back hand should end up in front of the solar plexus. For a *dō* cut, the back hand is on the hip and for a cut to *kote* it should be on the hip as well but slightly forward to your centre line.

Women have a tendency for passivity; this is why I decided to emphasise *tsuki* in order to make them more aggressive. The *tsuki* in these guidelines must be performed with full vigour and full mind. The back hand reaches the solar plexus and the *sori* of the blade should rotate when penetrating. My point is that you should not thrust using your hands, but rather indeed the whole body. I was inspired by *jūken-jutsu*. Bayonet techniques use a leaping footwork called *tobikomi*, but I chose to use instead *suriashi* and *fumikomi* when thrusting with the *naginata*.

Now, let us talk about the *ōyō* part of the guidelines.

Those patterns are quite practical, but it is important that the students should not deviate too far from what is taught. If one thinks that it is fine to focus on speed or softness, she would be making a big mistake. What is important here is to nullify the strength of your opponent then draw near, or to use your opponent's power in order to strengthen your own strike. Nullifying the opponent's strength is especially effective against *tsuki*; it is called *nayashi-ire-zuki*. In the last pattern, 17-*hon-me*, which was devised for normal school students, the attacker does consecutive cuts to the head and to the body. The defender blocks the strikes and gradually attracts her opponent; she eventually finishes off with a thrust. These are the kind of techniques that are in the *ōyō* section.

Regarding *harai* and *degashira* techniques; when performing a *harai*, one has to use the curve of the *naginata*'s *kissaki* and sweep her opponent's weapon downward. Also, one must rotate the *kissaki* from below towards where the opponent's front hand is the weakest. These are the important points when training in "*harai* then strike" exercises. *Harai* is not about merely slapping the opponent's weapon. The meaning of *harai* is to forbid the opponent starting another attack. No muscular strength is needed when attempting a *harai*, even a powerless person can perform a successful *harai* if she does it according to the principles. This is very important. Regarding *degashira*, it is crucial to pressure the source of the opponent's technique. *Degashira* is not a spiritless strike, but on the contrary a slash released in a flash. One should respond to the movements of her opponent's *kissaki* or front hand, and unleash her *naginata* at once.

Now, I would like to warn you about two or three points in the *ōyō* section that one can easily misunderstand.

First, *makiotoshi*. A *makiotoshi* technique can be very large or sometimes small. Depending on the way you perform *makiotoshi*, the ensuing *waza* may be affected and change accordingly. If you do a very large *makiotoshi*, the ensuing *tsuki* or cut or any move of the *naginata* might become difficult to perform. This is a critical point. In the guidelines, there is a pattern (*kata* No. 8) where one performs a *makiotoshi* on an incoming *hidari-men* cut, and finishes off with *tsuki*. This technique starts from *gedan*, so it is the largest *makiotoshi* of the whole series. Consequently, this has an impact on the ensuing *tsuki*: because the *makiotoshi* is extremely large, when performing the final thrust the back hand cannot go completely up to the solar plexus, but instead should rest in front of the lower abdomen. Secondly, there is a pattern called *tsuki ni tai suru makiotoshi*. The *makiotoshi* here should be smaller than the one in the previous case. At the end of a *makiotoshi*, one's *kissaki* should, as a norm, settle on her body's centre line. Therefore, in this pattern, one just has to rotate the *sori* of her blade, and thrust with her whole body; the back hand ends up in front of the solar plexus.

Let us talk about *mochikae*. Everybody tends to perform *mochikae* very quickly... It is indeed of some importance to be fast. However, when it comes to *mochikae*, accuracy is more essential than speed. Only when one has trained diligently on her accuracy, will she be able to become naturally fast. Students who have fast *mochikae* are generally the ones who perform uncompleted strikes. Therefore, instructors should always emphasise large and accurate *mochikae*.

When training in *kirikaeshi*, one should keep in mind a few points. *Kirikaeshi*'s pattern is as follows: *tsuki-tsuki-men-men-sune-sune*. It makes a rhythm, and it is easy to fall into that trap - I mean, to be caught by that rhythm. During *kirikaeshi*, after each *tsuki*, one has to pull her *naginata* back with strength, and at this very moment it is easy to end up with a crumbled posture. Also, one must remember to do large cuts and therefore perform large *mochikae*. If the *tenouchi* and the *tai-no-hiraki* are fully mastered, there will be no *suki* (opening). Thinking that there would be no opening in one's posture if performing a very quick *mochikae* is a big mistake. Even a slow *mochikae* should leave no *suki* for the opponent.

Finally, I really want to emphasise that an unbalanced, "light on the feet" unsettled posture is the worst thing to have. The whole body should settle in its centre. Flexibility and reactivity to all kinds of attacks is of course important; but your body should be filled with a spirit like a huge rock. However, having an immobile posture would also be wrong. An unperturbed posture is the key. I think that the posture called *shizentai* in judo is very important in naginata as well. This posture has not even a tiny bit of *suki*. Nevertheless, some may advocate that it is important to have the mental readiness that enables one to create a glimpse of *suki* in his posture and then to be able to react freely when the opponent is lured in to strike.

Sakakida (left) studying Tendō-ryū in Busen

To conclude, I would say that the essence is to polish a strong spirit, full of resolution, that can deal with everything that is coming at you.

Conclusion

In the three instalments on wartime naginata (*Kendo World* 6.3, 6.4 and the present issue), we saw different attempts to modernise the discipline into a unified curriculum. All three methods failed in their pursuit as they were either rejected or interrupted shortly after their inception. However, because it was certainly the most "official" of the three, being patronized by the Ministry of Education, and because it had severed the ties with the prominent naginata *ryūha* of the time and was a real evolution in terms of pedagogy, Sakakida Yaeko's method was eventually revived after the war, and transformed into a modern sport. The transition to the new naginata was supervised by Sakakida herself. She reused her *kihon* almost unchanged, but aggressive components such as the bayonet style thrusts were expurgated. The MSK were finally simplified and remoulded into the *shikake-ōji*, a set of basic movements still used nowadays to impart modern naginata techniques.

References.
- Gakuto Taiiku Kankōkai (ed.), "Naginata - Yōmoku no Seishin to sono Shidō", in *Gakuto Taiiku*, 1944.
- Ishigami, T. (ed.), "Yaeko, Ichizu ni Keiko Suru Hanashi", in *Kendo Nihon*, June & July 1982
- Monbushō, *Kokumin Gakkō Tairenka Budō (Naginata) Kyōju Yōkō, Chūtō Gakkō Tairenka Budō (Naginata) Kyōju Yōmoku, Shihan Gakkō Tairenka Budō (Naginata) Kyōju Yōmoku, Narabi ni Dō Kyōju Yōmoku (kō) Jisshi Saimoku*, republished in *Kindai Naginata Meicho Senshu 7*, Tokyo, Hon no Tomo-sha, 2004.

1本目 MEN NO ZANGEKI NI TAISHI UCHIOTOSHI-ZUKI

Guidelines:
From *chūdan* attack and cut *men*.
⇒ From *hidari-hassō* step back, perform *uchiotoshi* and thrust to *nodo* (throat).

Notes:
— This *kata* was studied from primary school, 6th grade.
— In the MSK, right or left stances are named after the position of the *naginata*: if the weapon is held on the left side of the body, then one is assuming a left stance or *hidari-kamae*. If the weapon is on the right side of the body, then one is assuming a right stance or *migi-kamae*. It is therefore the opposite of modern *shikake-ōji* where left or right stances are named after the foot that is in front.
Thus, in the first picture of this series, the practitioner on the left is assuming a *hidari-hassō*, with the *naginata* on her left side. In *shikake-ōji*, this kamae would be called *migi-hassō*, again because her right foot is in front.

2本目 SUNE NO ZANGEKI NI TAISHI NUKI MEN ZANGEKI

Guidelines:
From *hassō* attack and cut *sune*.
⇒ From *hassō* step back to avoid the *sune* cut, and cut to *men*.

Notes:
— This *kata* was studied from primary school, 6th grade.
— Even if the final *men* cut is performed from *hassō*, it is not a *soku-men* in this case but a *shōmen*. Therefore, the back hand rests below the abdomen at the end of the strike.

3本目 KOTE NO ZANGEKI NI TAISHI NUKI HIDARI-MEN ZANGEKI

Guidelines:
From *chūdan* attack and cut *kote*.
⇒ From *waki* step back diagonally to avoid the *kote* cut, and cut to *hidari-men*.

Notes:
— This *kata* was studied from middle school, 1st grade.
— Here, the final *men* cut is performed from *waki*, but it is not a *shōmen* strike. This is a *soku-men* cut (to the left) and thus, the back hand should rest in front of the solar plexus at the end of the strike.

4本目　TSUKI NI TAISHI MAKIOTOSHI-ZUKI

Guidelines:
From *chūdan* attack and thrust to *nodo*.
⇒ From *chūdan* step back and perform a *makiotoshi*, then thrust to *nodo*.

Notes:
— This *kata* was studied from middle school, 2nd grade.
— Apart from the bayonet style thrusts employed here, this pattern is similar to the first *kata* in modern naginata.

5本目 DŌ NO ZANGEKI NI TAISHI NUKI MEN ZANGEKI

Guidelines:
From *waki* attack and cut *dō*.
⇒ From *waki* step back to avoid the *dō* cut, and cut to *men*.

Notes:
— This *kata* was studied from middle school, 2nd grade.
— *Shikake-ōji* No. 8 uses elements of this pattern.

6本目　SUNE NO ZANGEKI NI TAISHI ŌJIKAESHI SUNE ZANGEKI

Guidelines:
From *hassō* attack and cut *sune*.
⇒ From *hidari-chūdan* step back and block the *sune* cut in *hidari-gedan* posture. Then perform an *ōjikaeshi* rotating to the right in order to cut *sune*.

Notes:
— This *kata* was studied from middle school, 2nd grade.
— *Ōjikaeshi* refers to a block followed immediately by a counter strike. It also implies the idea of an *uke-nagashi*; therefore, in this pattern, the defender should use the momentum given by the *sune* strike in order to perform his *ōjikaeshi-sune*.

7本目   DŌ NO RENZOKU ZANGEKI NI TAISHI NUKI HIDARI-MEN ZANGEKI

Guidelines:
From *waki* attack and cut *hidari-dō*.
⇒ From *hassō* step back and block the cut with the *shinogi* in *hidari-kamae*.

Then attack and cut *migi-dō*.
⇒ Step back with the right foot and avoid the cut in *migi-waki* fashion, but with the *ishizuki* raised higher than usual. Then cut *hidari-men*.

Notes:
— This *kata* was studied from middle school, 2nd grade.
— This pattern has become *shikake-ōji* No. 8. The only difference with the modern version resides in the last cut, which, in the MSK, is a *hidari-men* instead of a *shōmen*.

8本目　HIDARI-MEN NO ZANGEKI NI TAISHI MAKIOTOSHI-ZUKI

Guidelines:
From *hassō* attack and cut *hidari-men*.
⇒ From *hidari-gedan* step back and perform a *makiotoshi*, then thrust to *nodo*.

Notes:
— This *kata* was studied from middle school, 3rd grade.
— As stated by Sakakida Yaeko: "In the guidelines, there is a pattern where one performs a *makiotoshi* on an incoming *hidari-men* cut, and finishes off with *tsuki*. This technique starts from *gedan*, so it is the largest *makiotoshi* of the whole series. Consequently, this has an impact on the ensuing *tsuki*: because the *makiotoshi* is extremely large, when performing the final thrust the back hand cannot go completely up to the solar plexus, but instead should rest in front of the lower abdomen."

9本目 TSUKI NI TAISHI NAYASHI-IRE-ZUKI

Guidelines:
From *chūdan* attack and thrust to *nodo*.
⇒ From *chūdan* step back to "exhaust" (*nayashi*) the opponent's thrust, then close the gap (*irimi*) and thrust to *nodo*.

Notes:
— This *kata* was studied from middle school, 3rd grade.
— The concept of "*nayashi*" is studied in modern naginata through *kata* No. 1, where one exhausts his opponent's tsuki and then performs a *makiotoshi*. Here in the MSK, instead of a *makiotoshi*, the defender "enters" in his opponent's centreline (or "enters" the opponent's *waza*) and thrusts. This is a basic principle in Japanese bayonet fencing.

10本目 MEN NO ZANGEKI NI TAISHI ŌJIKAESHI KESA-GIRI

Guidelines:
From *hassō* attack and cut *men*.
⇒ From *chūdan* step back diagonally to the right, and block the cut in *jōdan* with the *shinogi*. Then perform *ōjikaeshi* and cut *kesa*.

Notes:
— This *kata* was studied from middle school, 3rd grade.
— This pattern is close to the final move of *kata* No. 6 in modern naginata (*uke-nagashi men*).

11本目　MEN NO ZANGEKI NI TAISHI MAKIOTOSHI KOTE NO MENGEKI

Guidelines:
From *hassō* attack and cut *men*.
⇒ From *chūdan* step back, perform a *makiotoshi* and cut *kote*. Immediately control the right side, rotate the *ishizuki* and strike *men*.

Notes:
— This *kata* was studied from middle school, 3rd grade.
— "Control the right side" (*migi ni seisuru*): close the gap so no strike can come to your right side anymore.

12本目 DŌ NO ZANGEKI NI TAISHI KURIKOMI MAKIOTOSHI MENGEKI

Guidelines:
From *waki* attack and cut *dō*.
⇒ From *chūdan* step back, pulling your *naginata* in, and block the *dō* cut with the *shinogi*. Immediately perform a *makiotoshi*, then rotate the *ishizuki* and strike *men*.

Notes:
— This *kata* was studied from middle school, 4th grade.

13本目 MEN NO ZANGEKI NI TAISHI NUKI DŌ ZANGEKI

Guidelines:
From *chūdan* attack and cut *men*.
⇒ From *waki* step back diagonally to the right to avoid the *men* cut, and cut *dō*.

Notes:
— This *kata* was studied from middle school, 4th grade.

14本目 KOTE NO ZANGEKI NI TAISHI ŌJIKAESHI HIDARI-MEN, ISHIZUKI TSUKI

Guidelines:
From *gedan* attack and cut *kote*.
⇒ From *hidari-jōdan* rotate the body to the right and block with the *shinogi*, then cut *hidari-men*.

Block the *hidari-men* cut with the *ishizuki*, and perform a *harai*.
⇒ Use the momentum of the *harai* to perform a thrust to the side with the *ishizuki*.

Notes:
— This *kata* was studied from middle school, 4th grade.
— There is no mention in the guidelines that the defender should assume the *kumi-ashi* posture before thrusting with the *ishizuki*, as it is done nowadays in *shikake-ōji* No. 6.

15本目 MEN NO ZANGEKI NI TAISHI ŌJIKAESHI SUNE, ŌJI HIDARI-MEN, HARAI ISHIZUKI TSUKI

Guidelines:

From *hassō* attack and cut *men*.
⇒ From *waki* raise *ishizuki* and block the *men* cut, then cut *sune*.

Block the *sune* cut with the *ishizuki*, and cut *hidari-men*.
⇒ Rotate the *ishizuki* and perform a *harai* to the right, then thrust to the side with the *ishizuki*.

Notes:
— This *kata* was studied from middle school, 4th grade.

16本目 HIDARI-MEN SUNE NO RENZOKU ZANGEKI NI TAISHI ŌJIKAESHI HIDARI-MEN, KAISEN KESA-GIRI

Guidelines:
From *jōdan* attack and cut *hidari-men*.
⇒ From *jōdan* move from the front foot to the left, rotate and block the *hidari-men* cut with the *shinogi*.

Immediately attack and cut *sune*.
⇒ Pull back the front foot and block the *sune* cut with the *ishizuki* in front of the body. Then cut *hidari-men*.

Block the *hidari-men* cut with the *ishizuki* and perform a *harai*.
⇒ Use the momentum of the *harai* and rotate the naginata to the right in order to cut *kesa*.

Notes:
— This *kata* was studied from normal school.

17本目 HIDARI-MEN MIGI-MEN DŌ NO RENZOKU ZANGEKI NI TAISHI KURIKOMI ŌJI TSUKI

Guidelines:

From *hassō* attack and cut *hidari-men*.
⇒ From *hassō* move from the front foot to the left and block the *hidari-men* cut with the *shinogi*.

Attack and cut *migi-men*.
⇒ Take a small step back, pull in the *naginata* (*kurikomi*) and block the *migi-men* cut with the *shinogi*.

Attack and cut *hidari-dō*.
⇒ Pull in the *naginata* and block the *hidari-dō* cut with the *shinogi*. Control the opponent's *naginata* on the left side, enter in close quarter and thrust to *nodo*.

Notes:

— This *kata* was studied from normal school.

PART 8
STRATEGY FOR NITŌ

By Yamaguchi Masato

1- Theory

Kamae

For *ittō* kendoka, the *shōtō* is the obstacle in controlling the *nitō* kendoka. The first step is to not let the *shōtō* work. Against the orthodox *kamae* of *chūdan* (*ittō*), it is very easy for the *nitō* player to gauge the *maai* and to push down the *shinai*. Therefore, one of the best *kamae* to take against *nitō* is *hira-seigan*, a *kamae* in which the *shinai* is held open. However, if the *kamae* is open too wide, the *nitō* kendoka will enter into your *maai*. Therefore, the key is to control the centreline. Open the *shinai* to the degree where the *nitō* player will have difficulty pushing down and attacking at the same time. It will also be impossible to control the *nitō* kendoka without *seme*.

In both orthodox and *gyaku-nitō*, if you direct your *shinai* to the outside of the *shōtō* or *daitō*, it will be easier for the *nitō* player to enter your *maai*. On the other hand, if you put your *shinai* on your centreline, it will be easier for them to hold your *shinai* down. The basic place to position your *shinai* is on the *nitō* player's centreline.

The reason why everybody worries about strategy when fighting against *nitō* kendoka is that few people know *nitō*'s centreline. As mentioned before, the centre of *nitō* is the middle of the two centres of gravity between the *daitō* and the *shōtō*. The line is shifted to the left (orthodox *nitō*) and the right (*gyaku-nitō*) from the viewpoint of the *ittō* kendoka. Therefore, even if the *ittō* kendoka puts their *shinai* on their centreline, it is a very good position for the *nitō* player to hold down the *shinai* with the *shōtō*. Therefore, you need to shift your centreline to the left or right by turning your body diagonally together with your *shinai*.

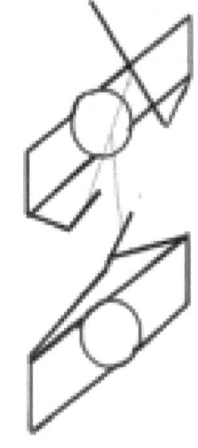

Figure 1
Fighting for control of the centreline (gyaku-nitō vs. hira-seigan)

Spatial Distances

As mentioned earlier, the short distance from which the *shōtō* can reach your *shinai* is one of the strengths of *nitō*. Know your own spatial distance well and do not fight in *nitō*'s. If *nitō* did not have the *shōtō*, it would only be one-handed *jōdan*. Additionally, with one hand, the *nitō* kendoka has to handle a 37 size *shinai*, which is about 6cm shorter than a 39. It is therefore advantageous to 'kill' the ability of the *shōtō* from the point of spatial distance. (Figure 2)

a

b

c

Figure 2 A comparison of maai: (a) chūdan (ittō), (b) jōdan (ittō), (c) jōge-tachi (nitō)

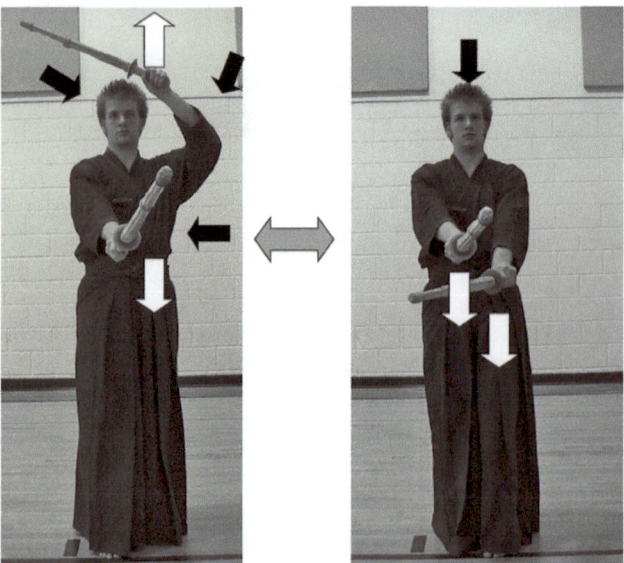

Figures 3 Shinai movements.

Side Changes

A *nitō* kendoka is good at attacking from either the right or left sides. However, the spaces in between changing become weak points, so aim at those. In the case where the *nitō* kendoka cannot change sides, you should attack from side to side. It will be easier for you to overwhelm this type of *nitō* kendoka. The following pictures illustrate *kote-nuki-men* (orthodox *nitō*). The body moves to the right side in the first picture, and then the body moves to the left in the third picture. (Figure 4) The moment that the sides change is the chance to strike. (Figure 5)

Figure 5 The space created in between changing sides.

Shinai movements

It is important to observe the *shinai* well because the movements of the two *shinai* are quite simple. Generally, a *nitō* kendoka's two *shinai* move in the same direction, which means that you can strike the areas that are open when they execute a strike. For example, *nitō* kendoka are trained to protect *men* after striking *kote*. In this moment, *dō* opens and is able to be struck. *Ittō* kendoka are familiar with striking *men* when responding to *kote* (*kote-nuki-men*), but you can strike any opening if you know the movements. (Figure 3)

Figure 4 Changing sides from right to left (orthodox nitō).

Awareness

It is important to be aware of both *shinai* when fighting a *nitō* kendoka. It is often said, "Don't pay attention to the *shōtō*." However, most *ittō* kendoka only focus on the *shōtō*. *Nitō* kendoka know this, which gives them a good chance to strike.

Balance

Breaking a *nitō* kendoka's balance is one method to use against them. For example, try to attack from the right side and then change to the left, or try to attack from the left and then feint and attack the centre. In short, you need to attack three parts at the same time. If the *ittō* kendoka has bad basics, their posture will also be broken when attacking.

Characteristics

If the orthodox *nitō* player has the right foot forward and the distance between the legs is wide, this means that they do not feel the twist in their body. In this case, the motion is easy to stop and they will be especially vulnerable to *tsuki*. The wide distance between the legs cannot cope with *seme* from side to side.

Techniques

Basic Strikes

1- Striking at the moment the opponent changes *kamae* (*kamae-giwa*)

When the *nitō* player starts or restarts a match, they change their *kamae* from *chūdan* to *jōge-tachi* in most cases. Aim for that moment of transition as halfway between the *kamae* is a weak point. *Nitō* players also understand this well, but this attack will be mentally effective. It is better to avoid striking *tsuki* and *kote* on the *shōtō* side. They can be easily parried, even if they are surprise strikes. (Figures 6~8)

Figure 6 Striking men at kamae-giwa.

Figure 7 Striking kote at kamae-giwa

Figure 8 Striking dō at kamae-giwa.

2. Striking at the moment the opponent moves to strike (*okori-gashira*)
   When the opponent's *shōtō* is not strong, aim to strike when they do. (Figures 9–11)

Figure 9 Striking kote at okori-gashira.

Figure 10 Striking men at okori-gashira.

Figure 11 Striking dō at okori-gashira.

3. Striking at the moment the opponent pulls back the *daitō* (*hiki-giwa*)
   Make the *nitō* player pull back their *daitō* with strong *seme*. After this, strike the opened area. (Figures 12 and 13)

Figure 12 Hiki-giwa dō strike.

Figure 13 Hiki-giwa men strike.

4. Striking at the moment the opponent cuts down with the *daitō* (*oroshi-giwa*)
   If you can suppress the *daitō* side, it will be easy to strike. (Figures 14 and 15)

Figure 14 Tsuki at oroshi-giwa.

Figure 15 Striking men at oroshi-giwa.

Renzoku-waza

1. Striking below and then up (*kote-kote - daitō side*)

Nitō players are good at responding to their opponent's strikes. Therefore, continuous strikes are more useful than single ones. Change their degree and speed depending on the opponent, which will give variation to your *seme*.

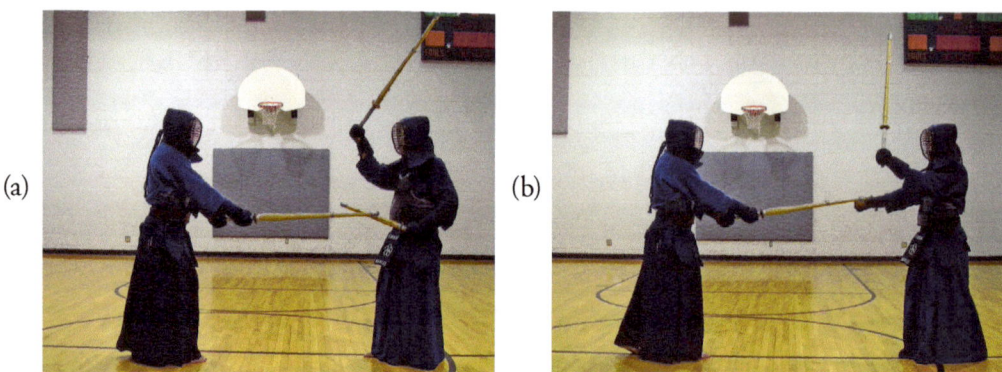

Figure 16 Methods of defending kote: (a) pulling back; (b) pushing down the shōtō.

When the *nitō* player pushes down his *shōtō* and defends, prepare and make a second strike. (Figure 17) If it is possible to strike *kote* on the *daitō* side, it will be highly advantageous. Because there are various methods of defending *kote*, observe the *nitō* player's habits well. You do not need to touch the *shōtō*, just make the *nitō* player move it. Note that attacks repeatedly made to the same side will be easily defended by the *nitō* player. (Figure 18)

Figure 17 Kote-kote (daitō side).

Figure 18 Kote-men strike.

2. Striking from below and then to the side (*kote-dō*)
Seme to make the *nitō* player move the *shōtō* and aim to strike at that moment. If your *seme* is not strong enough, your attack will be easily responded to. (Figure 19)

Figure 19 Kote-dō.

2. Striking forward and then up (*tsuki-men*)
After *seme*, *tsuki*. The *nitō* player will respond to it, and at that moment strike the opened areas. So as not to be controlled by the *shōtō*, dominate the *maai*. (Figure 20)

Figure 20 Tsuki-men.

Ōji-waza
This section will give some examples of *ōji-waza*. Each technique is based on the theories previously explained.

1. Against *men*.

Figure 21 Men-suriage-men.

Figure 22 Men-kaeshi-men.

Figure 23 Men-kaeshi-dō.

Figure 24 Kote-kaeshi-men.

2. Against *kote*

Figure 25 Kote-suriage-kote.

Figure 26 Kote-nuki-men.

3. Against *dō* and *tsuki*

Figure 27 Dō-uchiotoshi-men.

Figure 28 Tsuki-suriage-men.

R. A. Lidstone, circa 1927

R. A. Lidstone, circa 1963

'A MAN OF MANY PARTS'
Portrait of an Inimitable Swordsman

Ronald Alexander Lidstone (1895—1969)

Part 1: From Sea to Air—a Journey of 30 Years

By Paul Budden

The New Zealand newspaper, *NZ Truth*, Issue 1040, October 31, 1925:

"A MAN in his time plays many parts" said the poet. Such a one is Ronald Alexander Lidstone now at Auckland. Young in appearance, there's many a man would give something to have seen what he has, or travelled as much. His pie of life is full of meat. Trained for mercantile marine at Osbourne and Dartmouth he became a Lieutenant in the Navy in the Big War, and was on the Marlborough in the Battle of Jutland. Later he went to "Gay Paree," and followed the alluring profession of the light fantastic. Incidentally he polished up his knowledge of the fencing art. A master of the foil, sabre, single stick and quarterstaff, he can hold his own with any man. In New Zealand's first film, Rewi's Last Stand, he took the part of Von Tempsky with singular success".

However, even in 1925 the newspapers sometimes got their facts a little mixed up, as rather than the Merchant Navy it was actually in the Royal Navy that R. A. Lidstone saw service. After attending Lindesfarne School in Blackheath, London, his parents decided that Ronald should join the Royal Navy, quite in keeping with the way such decisions were made in those times. He was accepted in 1908 aged twelve and three quarters as a naval cadet and trained firstly at the Royal Naval College in Osbourne on the Isle of Wight for two years, and then at the Royal Naval College in Dartmouth, Devon. Two of the other cadets were Prince Edward (later King Edward VIII and the Duke of Windsor) and Prince Albert (later King George VI). There are recollections that a rough time was given to Prince Edward, especially in rugby lessons. "There was nothing personal, it was just who he was." His fellow cadets, including R.A. Lidstone, were also junior

R.A. Lidstone, circa 1913

HMS Marlborough

to him, and they were "most certainly up for it" with a capital C for "crunch".

As a Naval Cadet, RA, as we shall now refer to him, was introduced to swordplay and throughout the remainder of his life fencing, arms and armour were to be the greatest of all of his many interests. He would also later develop this as a profession. He competed three times at the Royal Navy and Military Tournament in Olympia, London: in 1911 as an under-16 cadet representing the Royal Naval College (sabre vs. sabre), in 1913 as a midshipman representing HMS Superb (sabre vs. sabre), and in 1914, again as a midshipman (bayonet vs. bayonet).

Throughout World War I (1914-1918), RA served with the Grand Fleet on HMS Marlborough as an acting Sub-Lieutenant in charge of a gun turret. HMS Marlborough was a battleship of the Iron Duke class and was the flagship of Vice-Admiral Burney, and it was under the command of Admiral Sir John Jellicoe at the battle of Jutland. During that battle HMS Marlborough was hit by an enemy torpedo; fortunately the Marlborough did not sink and was able to continue with the engagement.

From the Lidstone family records:

"At 6.45pm on the 31st the Marlborough was hit by a torpedo amidships and had a 70ft x 70ft hole blown in her side plating. In spite of that she kept station at 17 knots still firing at the enemy. She was now settling somewhat from the effects of the torpedo hit, several compartments around the hit flooded and at 2am on the 1st June she was directed to return to port which she did, Vice-Admiral Burney having transferred his flag to HMS Revenge".

At the end of the Great War, RA resigned his commission and in 1919 he met his future wife, Isolde, a professional dancer who performed adagio (acrobatics). Isolde needed a new dancing partner, and failing to find one with the qualifications she required, Isolde sought the help of her brother, Brettoner, a wartime officer in the Royal Flying Corps. He posted an advert on the notice board of an ex-officer's club and "Ronald Alexander Lidstone Lieut. RN Retired" applied, even though he had no stage or dancing experience, could not sing or had done any "lifts" - which was a specific requirement. However, he confidently expressed that he was capable of learning and was prepared to show that his "conviction was not boasting". He was successfully accepted and together they "trod the boards" becoming the successful adagio dancing duo *"Isolde and Alexis"*. They made a name for themselves as a dance and musical act appearing at top London theatres and cabarets, as well as touring throughout the UK, Paris and South Africa. Three months after he had auditioned they were engaged to be married. On hearing of the engagement, Isolde's mother sent her a telegram saying "Congratulations and blessings, exactly to my taste".

There is a Pathe News clip from 1936 showing them together, R. A. lifting Isolde whilst she plays the mandolin without interruption.

With classical routines like the Tango and Apache[1] the dances were interspersed with "fencing to music" making up their repertoire. The productions were both exciting and entertaining, such was their unique if somewhat

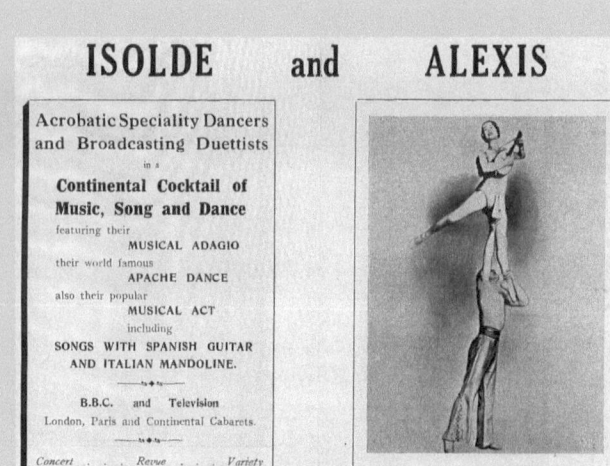

Flyer, circa 1930

Stage fencing, circa 1925

unorthodox versatility. On one occasion whilst dancing the Apache, Isolde was thrown across the floor and hit her head against a table leg which was made of iron, knocking her unconscious. Alexis picked her up carrying her off across his shoulder with the audience none the wiser thinking this just part of the act. Later the duo sometimes appeared as a trio when various musicians and entertainers were engaged, with musical sketches introduced for the variety stage.

This from their eldest daughter Joan Childs:

Apache Dance, circa 1928

"Imagine yourself on a night out at the Café de Paris, the smartest night spot in London (where Noel Coward, Marlene Dietrich, Gertrude Lawrence and many other famous stars appeared). From your table you can see two grand staircases swirling gracefully down either side of the bandstand to the dance floor. At the top of the stairs Alexis has just Lifted Isolde onto his shoulder, her mandolin held safely, and the couple are now descending slowly to the floor where their unique Acrobatic Mandolin Dance will begin. All is glamour and glory".

But these enchanting moments were only part of the story as sometimes there was no work, and they struggled with financial insecurity over many years. What prompted the next move is not exactly clear, but after returning to England from a short tour of South Africa, and with uncertainties seemingly lying ahead, they made the decision to emigrate. They left England in 1924 based on an offer from a naval friend who had already emigrated to New Zealand. He was keen to set up a Timber business and suggested that RA should join him there. Both he and Isolde were enthusiastic about the idea and off they went to New Zealand. Unfortunately, the business came to nothing, and struggling for money, RA took a position as "Sports Master" in charge of physical fitness at St. Patrick's College. There he also taught fencing, physical culture and dancing together with Isolde. To try and make ends meet, they toured again as Isolde and Alexis, eventually with limited success.

During this time, he arranged the sword fights and starred in the first silent film made in New Zealand, *Rewi's Last Stand*, using the stage name Charles Alexis. This came from being known as Charles to stage colleagues and friends, and his dancing name, Alexis, which itself was taken from his second name, Alexander, and was

On set

Kendo display, Wellington Harbour, 1932

Poster for Rewi's Last Stand 1925

Dance and fencing Studio Sydney, 1926

Fencing Display, circa 1923

used due to the belief that in those days the best dancers were Russian.

It was in New Zealand that RA first witnessed kendo whilst living in Auckland. The Japanese naval ship Iwate was visiting in February 1926 as part of a training voyage throughout the Pacific (the Iwate was also to visit again in 1932[2]). The crew put on a show of their national martial arts. RA was both intrigued and fascinated by the kendo display and this would have a lasting effect on him throughout his life.

In order to try and improve their ever problematic financial situation, RA and Isolde moved to Sydney, Australia, in 1926. They opened a dance and fencing studio as well as RA being "Instructor of Fencing & Physical Culture" at the Dupain Institute of Physical Education and the "Swords Club", and also working for Phonofilms.

Their real dream, however, was to return home to England, but the constant lack of funds dictated that they could never even consider affording the fares. In 1928

RA's Aunt Mary died leaving a small legacy, and they were able to book passage back to England. On their return, RA joined a film unit agency called "The Stunt Club" in London and took what work it offered him. He also took up kendo at the Anglo Japanese Jujutsu and Martial Arts Association under Mishiku Kaoru-sensei. In 1909 Mishiku-sensei had arrived in London and very quickly took over the running of the Anglo Japanese Jujutsu and Martial Arts Association at the new dojo in Strathmore Gardens, London. A graduate of the Butokukai's school Busen, the premier martial arts college in Japan, Mishiku-sensei was a master of judo, jūjutsu and kendo. He employed various other Japanese masters including Okamoto Yoshitomo-sensei whom RA credits with his initial instruction [3].

Together with members of the recently renamed Anglo Japanese Judo Club in London, Okamoto Yoshitomo-sensei and Mishiku Kaoru-sensei demonstrated some *koryū kata* as part of a kendo display at the Holborn Stadium in front of Lady Curtis-Bennett [4] in 1936. R.A. Lidstone was also promoted to the rank of 6-kyu, the *menjō* being signed by Okamoto, Kuzutani and Mishiku in that same year.

The fascinating description of now being permitted to wear "the yellow belt and white *hakama*" paints a rather interesting picture together with the advice:

> *"FOR YOUR PRIVATE INFORMATION. Please remember that the secret of success in kendo is courage and to train yourself to always before you receive a scratch to give a 'Flesh-Cut', and before you receive a 'Flesh-Cut' to give a 'Bone–Cut'. In other words, always anticipate with interest your opponent's tactics".*

In May 1937, he was selected to take part in a kendo demonstration for Prince Chichibu at a garden party held in his honour at the Hurlingham Sports Club, Fulham, London. This was with members of the Anglo Japanese Judo Club who organised the event. Those taking part included Fukima, Kuzutani Arataro, Koizumi Gunji,

The Stunt Club film agency London. Lidstone is on the left with pipe in mouth, circa 1930

Mishiku-sensei in Japan, date unknown

Holborn Stadium display, 1936. Okamoto-sensei (l), Mishiku-sensei (r)

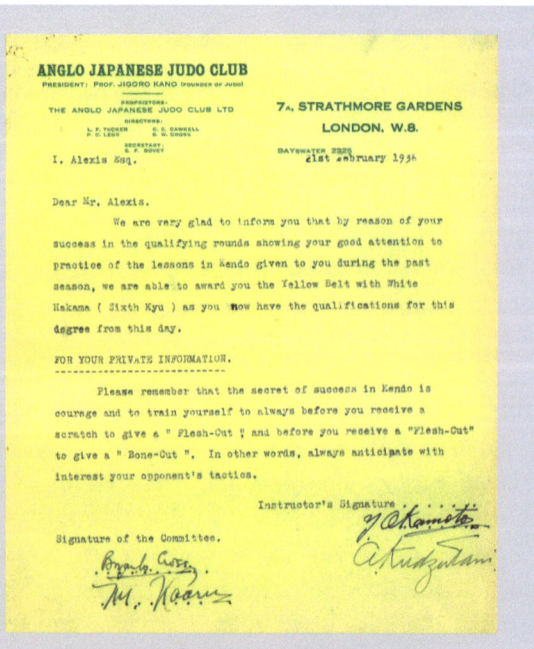

Lidstone's menjō, 1937

Sakakibara, Omori, Okamoto Yoshitomo, Mishiku Kaoru, Nogi, Calmer, R.A. Lidstone, Fenlon, Rudwell, Cope, Hanibourn, Pepler and Philips.

This from *An Introduction to Kendo*:[5]

"When Prince Chichibu visited England in 1937 a garden party was given at Hurlingham in his honour and for his entertainment sixteen kendoka from the Anglo-Japanese Judo Club put on an uchi-majiri (a type of contest but more literally translated as a brawl or melee). On this occasion we had hard biscuits tied on our armour at the vulnerable points and these had to be broken before we were considered maketa (defeated). As it was impossible for us to tell if ours had been broken or not the judges had to rush in amongst the flaying shinai and pull the 'dead' ones out!"

As early as 1926, RA had begun writing and his two books on fencing, although out of print, remain an authoritative treatise on the subject. *Bloody Bayonets*, written whilst serving in the RAF and published in 1942, became the unofficial handbook to the armed forces during World War II.[6] *An Introduction to Kendo* was the first book ever written in English on kendo and it contained illustrations by Roald Knutsen and photographs by Alan R. Menzies.

Interestingly his first publications from 1926, a fascinating series on symbology, have now been reissued.

RA contributed many articles to *The Sword*, a fencing magazine. Roy Goodall, the editor, referred to him as "this great man" and "the outstanding authority in the country on the history of fencing". RA was in touch with most of the important figures in the fencing world and in 1968 was invited to edit and write a foreword to Egerton Castle's book, *Schools and Masters of Fence from the Middle Ages to the Eighteenth Century* (1969).

When fears that a war with Germany was likely in 1937, RA joined the Corps of Volunteers (a voluntary body formed to deal with air raid precautions). After training, he was made Staff Captain. Early in 1939 he went to Nottingham working there as a civilian for the RAF in their codes and ciphers department. When war finally came in September of that year, he was conscripted into the RAF and made a Flight Lieutenant. With a powerful intellect that would tackle most problems, both mental and physical, RA was often moved to quote Lord Nelson's motto before tackling any particularly demanding test, "There is nothing the Navy cannot do". A form of shorthand, an ingenious chord finder as an aid to musicians, a braking system for cars[8] and a water heater[9] were innovations that he created.

Throughout World War II, RA continued to serve as an officer in the Royal Air Force and reached the rank of Squadron Leader. He had various postings including being stationed at Leighton Buzzard, Bedfordshire, where he wrote his complete guide to bayonet fighting, *Bloody Bayonets*. Towards the end of the war, he was concerned with the handing over to the British of a number of American Air Force bases, for which he was granted the

Hurlingham Garden Party display, 1937

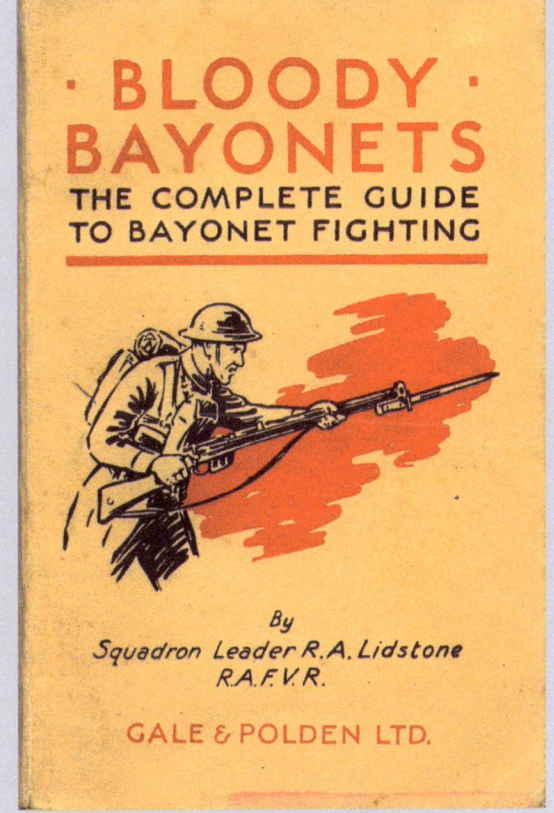

Bloody Bayonets 1942

Preparing the sketch positions for **Bloody Bayonets**, *circa 1942*

temporary rank of Wing Commander, reverting back to Squadron Leader on his discharge.

Meticulous and fair in dealing with others, he was always considerate and courteous with a gentle sense of humour, though he did not suffer fools gladly. Put quite simply, he was a complete gentleman of the old school.

This article will continue in the next edition of *Kendo World*, and will look at RA's life after World War II.

References and Background Sources
- 'Ronald' & 'Isolde' books compiled and written by David Lidstone and Joan Childs (née Lidstone)
- The Alexander Turnbull Library New Zealand
- John Bowen, the personal records of his late brother Richard Bowen 'Judo History'
- The British Newspaper Archive
- The Budokwai 'Judo History Records'
- British Pathe
- Roald and Pat Knutsen, personal records
- The National Library of New Zealand and Papers Past
- Frank Perry and the 'Bu'sen Martial Arts School, London
- Wikipedia

Acknowledgements
I would like to thank Brian Lidstone, his wife Jenny and members of the Lidstone Family, Roald and Pat Knutsen, John Bowen, Kazuyo Matsuda, Terry Holt, Ian Parker Dodd and Frank Perry for their invaluable information, generous assistance and great kindness.

Endnotes
1. From Wikipedia: Apache, or La Danse Apache, Bowery Waltz, Apache Turn, Apache Dance and Tough Dance is a highly dramatic dance associated in popular culture with Parisian street culture at the beginning of the 20th century. The name of the dance (pronounced *ah-PAHSH*, not *uh-PATCH-ee*, like the English pronunciation of the Native American tribe) is taken from the term for Parisian underworld of the time. The dance is sometimes said to re-enact a violent "discussion" between a pimp and a prostitute. It includes mock slaps and punches, the man picking up and throwing the woman to the ground, or lifting and carrying her while she struggles or feigns unconsciousness. Thus, the dance shares many features with the theatrical discipline of stage combat. In some examples, the woman may fight back.
2. Japanese sailors entertain Wellingtonians with a display of martial arts on Pipitea Wharf beside the warship Asama. Photographed by an *Evening Post* staff photographer June 2, 1932. The occasion was the visit of a Japanese naval training squadron to Wellington, New Zealand. The two warships were the Asama and the Iwate. From Wellington the squadron sailed to Suva, Fiji. Picture Courtesy of the Alexander Turnbull Library, New Zealand, reference number 1/2-121102-G.
3. Lidstone, R.A. *An introduction to Kendo*, (Charles Alexis), Judo Limited, Croydon. 1964.
4. British Pathe 1936: http://www.britishpathe.com/video/judo-and-kendo/query/kendo
5. Lidstone, R.A. *An introduction to Kendo*, op.cit.
6. Lidstone, R.A. *Bloody Bayonets: The Complete Guide to Bayonet Fighting*, Gale & Polden Ltd., Aldershot. 1942.
7. 'In *Bloody Bayonets* published in 1942 title listings page Squadron Leader R.A Lidstone is noted as the author of "*Kendo: The Art of Japanese Swordsmanship*" which implies that a preliminary version under a different title had been produced before 1940 and possibly as early as 1936: This is also indicated in the Lidstone personal archive notes. To date we have not been able to trace any copies of this publication.
8. *The Autocar* June 14,1935, "Two Controls in One"—'The Cave' a method of combining the brake & accelerator in cars. Although patented and with a prototype produced, it was never taken up by car manufacturers.
9. 'The Lighting Water Heater' manufactured by S.M Wilmot of Bristol in 1937. This was an idea that they brought back with them from Australia where a newspaper was put into an aluminium cylinder at the bottom of a barrel of cold water. The newspaper would then be lit and in no time there was enough hot water for a bath—a bath for a penny, as that was the average cost for a daily newspaper at that time.

An Oasis of Equality in the Male-Dominated World of Sport?
Finnish Women's Experience of Kendo

By Rita Dekšnytė

I have enjoyed kendo because at the dojo, gender really doesn't matter. You can leave the outer world and all gender expectations outside and just focus on the main thing—practising—and nothing else.

—Laura, study participant

This article will introduce some of the findings of a qualitative research study aimed at exploring the experiences of three highly skilled Finnish female kendo athletes. It will focus on one of the themes emerging from the data, "the sports context", and discuss the ways that the kendo sports framework and culture mediates women's experiences.

Background

Gender equality in sports is a hot topic today. Hegemonic masculinity has been defining the world of sport for a long time, and despite the fact that women have been actively entering athletics, coaching, management, spectatorship and sports journalism, they are continuously being marginalised. We often hear that sport is a human right and "every individual must have the possibility of practising sport, without discrimination of any kind".[1] However, this human right remains largely not implemented as stereotypes and prejudice continue to discourage many women from physical activity altogether. There is something fundamentally wrong with the world of sport, and in order to tackle it, we need to look deeper into human experiences within sport. In this case, I am offering an insight into Finnish women's experiences of kendo.

Context

"It is difficult to talk about gender equality with Finnish women, simply because they have nothing to say, since they take it for granted," said my thesis supervisor when I expressed my wish to study Finnish women's experiences in kendo. Indeed, Finland is the leading country in the world in terms of gender equality [2] as well as gender equality in sports participation.[3] Therefore, it provided an exciting and challenging context in which to study women's experiences of kendo, a Far Eastern martial art, which, at least at first sight, looks nowhere near "feminine". I must admit, I did not choose kendo accidentally, but because I had recently started practising it, and I was very curious to hear from women with more experience.

Method

The qualitative research project aimed at exploring and understanding the experiences of three highly skilled Finnish female kendo athletes and shedding light on their personal and social meanings of gender and sport. To enable the participants to express their thoughts about the topic freely, the study adopted an open perspective. The three women were asked to write a reflective text in their own time according to the following prompt: "A woman in kendo. Reflect on your experience and write a story." To gain deeper insights, they were then asked to elaborate on some aspects of their texts as well as comment on each other's stories. The rich textual data was analysed, interpreted and categorised according to the emerging themes.

Findings

The open approach to data collection revealed a wide range of themes, which were categorised under four key titles: the personal, the socio-cultural, gender, and sports context. In this article I want to focus mainly on the sports context. More specifically, on how a kendo sports framework (goals, rules, norms) and culture mediates women's experiences.

A Tool for Personal Development?

Although the participants initially started kendo for different reasons, some purely by accident, others in search of something different to their prior sporting experience, kendo's focus on holistic personal development was what made them stay and sustain practice for many years.

Kendo is a tool to understand myself, how I learn, how I react to different people, different situations and how I handle pressure… I am still in the process of learning. (Silvia)

Kendo is valued by participants because it provides an opportunity to challenge themselves and others and develop new skills and competencies, such as self-esteem, determination and mental resilience. It is also a space for participants to face their own emotions and understand themselves better.

Somehow it felt that after every practice I had beat myself… That is the most challenging part—actually challenging yourself—facing all the emotions, good and bad. Also those emotions that you didn't really know you had in you. I think that I learn always something more about myself. (Eva)

This learning seems to be continuous, a life-long learning, and this potential quality of kendo is what motivates participants to continue practising. In fact, kendo has been contrasted with other sports, where athlete careers end very early.

Have you even heard of a female gymnast or figure skater, who continues her sport after her teens? (Silvia).

Furthermore, the skills and competencies developed through kendo are transferred to other areas of life, having a significant impact on participants' lives outside of the dojo, and helping them tackle challenges in daily life.

Focusing to see the opponent's attacks, the time to react, and the time to attack before them… I feel that it's all time within me. It's there when I'm walking in a crowd; facing people… I never know what kind of people they are, so I have to find a way to get in contact with them. I try to trust my instincts. (Eva)

A Gender-Neutral Sport?

Kendo was perceived by the participants as sport where men and women could practise together without prejudice, and this was, in a way, a relief for some participants who, despite living in a very equal society, have had experiences of gendered interactions in sport and life.

I have enjoyed kendo because at the dojo, gender really doesn't matter. You can leave the outer world and all gender expectations outside and just focus on the main thing—practising—and nothing else. (Laura)

The gender-equality of kendo emerged among other equalities. Participants valued the possibility to practise together regardless of gender, age, body size and shape,

skill level or language spoken. What plays a key role in this equality and openness of kendo is the focus on mental aspects rather than physical, and the focus on the previously discussed personal development.

> *It is the feeling that you're actually against yourself, your own mind and expectations. It doesn't really matter with whom you are practising, you always practise yourself and your own mind. (Eva)*

Equipment and outfit that is the same for everyone and does not reveal skill level was mentioned as one of the aspects preventing prejudice among the participants and even challenging them to develop an open mindset.

> *One doesn't see from the outfit any difference in if the practitioner has just started practising kendo or if he/she has practised for several years…That is also something interesting. To investigate the mind of your own if you have made some prejudice. (Eva)*

Finally, the key point facilitating positive women's experiences of kendo was with respect to fellow practitioners and opponents. Respect was seen as a key value, deeply ingrained in the philosophy of sport. Kendo was contrasted with other sports, that, although they declare respect as an ideal, often lack this value in practice.

> *You do not simply bow before and after a match because it's an empty ritual. You bow out of respect. Even if you lose, you bow to your opponent for teaching you an important lesson in losing. If you win, you do not throw your shinai around and do cartwheels, you contain yourself and thank your opponent for a good match. This is something that has always appealed to me in kendo which I have never found in any European sport I've tried. (Silvia)*

What is also evident in this quote is that kendo focuses on the process, as opposed to the result. Here the concept of respect connects with that of personal development. In other words, the opponent is seen as an enabler in one's personal development, challenging him or her and helping them to excel.

Women in Finnish Kendo and Cultural Challenges

Although participants' experiences depicted the kendo sports framework as facilitating non-gendered interactions, it is important to consider another mediator—the sociocultural context. In this case we can observe the interaction of the Finnish culture native to the participants and the Japanese culture native to kendo.

Participants expressed pride in Finnish women's achievements in kendo in the international arena, as well as pride in the significant role of women in the development of Finnish kendo. As Laura suggests, "These strong women have opened the path and women have become an essential part of Finnish kendo."

Our kendo society is built in a very "Finnish" way, where women carry a great deal of the burden of organising. We actually like talking about the "strong Nordic woman"... We are proud of this strength that we seem to possess and especially, if strangers notice and wonder about it. (Eva)

In the above quote, the awareness of cultural differences has already become evident. It becomes even more evident when women talk about gendered cultural encounters within a kendo context, expressing their disappointment for not being valued for their effort due to their gender.

I've always been a little insulted, when I've gone to so much trouble arranging something like a kendo seminar, and our Japanese guests shower their gratitude at the nearest guy they can find to thank, and seem to overlook my efforts altogether. (Eva)

It is clear that national culture influences the experiences of women in kendo in different ways, and cultural encounters pose challenges. However, even unpleasant cultural experiences are seen as a learning experience for both parties.

When Japanese men come to Finland without any former experience of kendo outside of Japan, they are sometimes a bit puzzled. Some of them accept and adapt to a situation, but some just can't understand and learn... For me it hasn't been a big problem. There have been a few Japanese men who had difficulties to get along with women, but from my point of view, with cultural encounters both sides should learn something like they do in keiko. (Laura)

Participation encourages both parties in cultural encounters to remember the values of kendo and, with respect and an open mind, practise accepting personal differences.

Conclusion

Although qualitative research studies such as this one do not offer generalisations of their findings, they seek to bring the reader closer to significant aspects of the general situation through a focus on the individual experience. I believe that some readers will realise how much he or she actually shares with these three Finnish women.

It does seem that the kendo sports framework —including its focus on mental aspects rather than physicality; personal development rather than winning; emphasis on respect to one's opponent; and prejudice-preventing attire—provides a gender-neutral environment where men and women can practise together and focus on what really matters: the practice itself. It also seems that other sports have a lot to learn from kendo. Therefore, I encourage all practitioners to promote kendo's good practices, not only for advocating gender equality, but for respect in general, to everyone in all areas of life.

However, the present study also raises a lot of questions. For example: Where does sporting culture end and national culture begin? How can other sports improve their framework to become more inclusive? Again, I encourage all readers, whether researchers or practitioners, to look for answers and share their findings with the wider community. I believe that through sharing ideas, we will make not only kendo, but sport in general, a better place for everyone.

End notes

1. International Olympic Committee, "Olympic Charter", (2013), p. 11, <www.olympic.org>
2. J. Plantenga, C. Remery, H. Figueiredo, & M. Smith, "Towards a European Union gender equality index", *Journal of European Social Policy*, (Vol. 19, No. 1, (2009), pp.19—33.
3. C. Van Tuyckom, J. Scheerder, & P Bracke, "Gender and age inequalities in regular sports participation: A cross-national study of 25 European countries", *Journal of Sports Sciences*, (Vol. 28, No. 10, 2010), pp. 1077-1084

About the author:

Rita Dekšnytė holds a double Master's degree in Sport and Exercise Psychology from the University of Jyväskylä (Finland) and the University of Leipzig (Germany). She is currently working as a sport psychology consultant in her home country of Lithuania. Her key research interest is gender identity construction in sport.

Contact details:
rita@sportpsycholo.gy
www.sportpsycholo.gy
www.deksnyterita.wordpress.com

BOOK REVIEW

By Charlie Kondek

I've read a lot of books to my children and other kids in my life, and if you've done the same, you know they will ask you to re-read their favorites. Repeatedly. It's always my hope as a parent, relative or mentor that the books they really gravitate to impart good lessons as well as entertain. Marco Garcia of Texas, USA, a youth coach in karate and a kendo—and *iaidoka* himself— has written just such a book, something you'll be proud to read to your kids and gladly pass on to others'.

GoGo Ninja concerns the frustrations of the title character as he tries to excel at soccer. Told in rhyme to an audience intended to be ages five and up (though I know kids younger might dig it), the tale follows GoGo from the soccer field to the dojo, where he laments to his sensei, "I think it may be best if I hang up my shoes. I don't want to play if all I do is lose."

Donning *bōgu*, the sensei guides GoGo through rigorous kendo training in which he is told, "Life is a battle. You must maintain control, discipline yourself, learn how to grow." Through continual emphasis on "Eye contact! Posture! Commitment without fear," GoGo attains his focus and enthusiasm once again. "The lesson from kendo had finally set in. You must have a plan, and the discipline to win."

Garcia says his ideas for his books—*GoGo Ninja* is the first of several—come from the years of his journaling in the martial arts, and are distillations of the lessons passed on to him by his various sensei, lessons he wants to pass on to others. "My goal is to bring awareness to future generations, that we all have a role to play in the quality of our accomplishments," he said. "Creating opportunity is the first step to reaching our true potential in life."

While I admired the book for its readability and the excellent artwork by Manuela Soriani, I did ask Garcia the orthodox kendo question of why the first GoGo book didn't focus on *rei*. "There are so many directions the book could have gone," he said. "My goal was to ensure that a single concept or message would be understood. For this reason *rei* is not specifically mentioned in text. However, the illustrations were edited in great detail to represent the traditional dojo and kendo lifestyle. *Rei* is illustrated and visible when GoGo arrives at the dojo and greets the sensei. This was the only way to ensure the message stayed on track."

He's right. The book demonstrates its message ably, which is a very effective way of teaching children. And, it's the kind of character and situation kids love, in a fun, rhyming style. Exactly the type of thing you as an adult might read… twice… three times… before finally insisting the child turn the light off and go to bed!

- Amazon-Kindle-Ebook—$4.99
- Apple-ibook-Ebook—$4.99
- Amazon Soft Cover—$13.99
- Amazon Hard Cover—$22.99
- Apple Itunes-Coloring book App—$4.99 (Estimated)

what is Tornado-stitch®?

- Innovative patented design
- Enhanced protection

- Correct angle of strike immediately visible
- Perfect for Kendo instructors

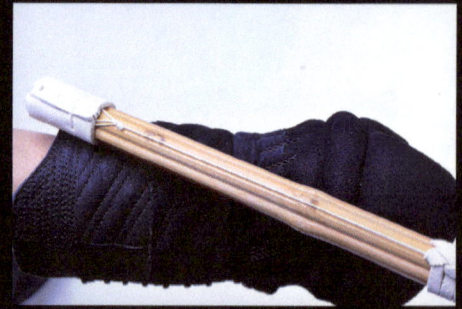

- Improved wrist mobility
- Available in indigo-dyed deerskin and orizashi cotton.

Read the whole story about the Tornado Stitch® and see our interview with the All Japan Kendo Federation Vice President, Mr. Fukumoto Shuji, about the advantages of the Tozando Tornado Stitch® Kote at www.Tozandoshop.com

Tornado-stitch® (Patent pending 2014-4504)

Tornado-stitch Indigo-dyed deerskin model

Tornado-stitch® (Patent pending 2014-4504)

Tornado-stitch Orizashi model

Tornado-stitch®, recommended for instructors, true to the essence of Kendo

The Shinai is a Sword. When you think of it like that, the concept of "Hasuji" becomes clear. "To strike with spirit, using the correct posture, hitting the target with the correct "Hasuji", following through with proper Zanshin". This is what is stated in the All Japan Kendo Federation Shiai and Referee Regulations. Also, "To strike with Spirit, Sword and Body as one", this is something that anyone practicing Kendo has to strive for while

Being aware of this, we listened to the voices of kendo instructors. They would ask for a Bogu that would perfectly protect when hit, while being exceptionally durable - all this would make teaching the correct Hasuji and playing Motodachi easier for them. To answer these requests, we kept researching and developing the possibilities for years, going through several prototypes in the process. As a result, by radically modifying the stitching method, we finally managed to create a unique Kote-buton, excellent in absorbing impact. The Tozando Tornado-stitch® was born.

We got an opportunity to show this innovative Kote to Mr. Fukumoto, the vice president of the All Japan Kendo Federation. "To be able to strike with the correct angle, this is the most important and critical difference of these Kote". These Kote both teach the essence of Kendo, making it easy to understand the concept of the sword's "Hasuji", and allow the instructor to receive the strikes safely.

The Tornado-stitch® Kote are made in our factory in Iwate prefecture under strict quality requirements. They are made by our craftsmen, who use all of their skills and heart, to make them one of the few "Made in Japan" Kote left on the market today. We are certain that these Tornado-stitch® Kote, used and loved by many Kenshi around the world, will become a true pillar of the promotion and the diffusion of strong and correct Kendo.

Tozando Co.,Ltd.
www.tozando.com